A Letter for My Mther

A Letter for My Mther

An Anthology
EDITED BY **Nina Foxx**

SBI
STREBOR BOOKS
NEW YORK LONDON TORONTO SYDNEY

Strebor Books
P.O. Box 6505
Largo, MD 20792
http://www.streborbooks.com

This book is a work of nonfiction. Certain names have been changed.

© 2014 *A Letter for My Mother* edited by Nina Foxx

ISBN 978-1-59309-532-1
ISBN 978-1-4767-4401-8 (ebook)
LCCN 2013950688

First Strebor Books trade paperback edition April 2014

Cover design: www.mariondesigns.com
Cover photograph: © Keith Saunders/Marion Designs

10 9 8 7 6 5 4 3 2 1

Manufactured in the United States of America

For information regarding special discounts for bulk purchases, please contact Simon
& Schuster Special Sales at 1-866-506-1949 or business@simonandschuster.com

The Simon & Schuster Speakers Bureau can bring authors to your live event. For
more information or to book an event, contact the Simon & Schuster Speakers Bureau
at 1-866-248-3049 or visit our website at www.simonspeakers.com.

In memory of my mother, Elvie Jackson Powell
And for Lynda A. Scott.
Thank you for being my mother, my sister and my friend.

Table of Contents

Introduction
by Nina Foxx

My ex-husband's mother was dying. During the time I was married to him, our relationship had been at best, tenuous. I married her oldest son and she never forgave me for that, or at least it seemed that way in my head. I couldn't seem to understand some of her ways and she couldn't understand mine. I was from a different place than she and my life was different than both hers and that of her daughters. At times, she seemed to resent me for that. Some days, she went from insulting me, my family, my upbringing and lifestyle in one sentence to embracing me and trying to nurture me, all in the space of a twelve-hour period. It was infuriating. I retaliated, resisted, rebelled and refused to accept. I'd already had a mother. She'd died when I was six, and no one could replace her. Various female members of my biological family had given me all the mothering I thought I would need so I saw no need to accept any from a stranger.

Over the years, our relationship changed and softened, especially after the children came, but I'll admit I was never comfortable with her. When I divorced her son, I thought I was walking away from her family too and struggled with the link that lay between us and the desire to do the right thing. I was more compelled to stay in contact with family than my ex-husband was, but didn't want to overstep my bounds by staying in touch with his family for my children. Divorce was a relationship quagmire I had a hard time negotiating. I wanted my children to know and love their family, all of it, but I didn't want to be the uncomfortable bridge that made that happen. My mother-in-law didn't care what I felt. She was always going to be here, and though my last name had changed, she still offered her opinion, advice and whatever else she felt like when we spoke, making me still more uncomfortable.

I knew she was ill, but I still felt as if I'd been knocked off my feet when I received the call that she was dying. Tears and confusion flooded my brain. At first, I couldn't understand why I was not emotionless. My sister, the main mother figure in my life, explained my reaction to me and encouraged me to tell my mother-in-law what I had to say to her before I no longer could. She assured me that even though I was unwilling to admit it, I was close to this woman and couldn't avoid being unnerved. We had developed a relationship over the years. My sister encouraged me to write down what I wanted to say to the woman before she died if I was unable to speak the words. The result was the letter that led to this book. As I wrote, I realized that although she and I were very different, my mother-in-law had been mothering me all along and didn't care whether I wanted to accept it or not. Because I had been raised to do the right thing, I started out treating her with respect, and even though my respect was peppered with defiance, it didn't stop me from loving her. Over time, I treated her with respect not because I was supposed to, but because I had come to respect her.

I finished my letter and my mother-in-law died three hours later. I was as devastated as if she had given birth to me, but I did feel some relief that I had said to the universe the things I wanted to say but hadn't been able to for the fifteen years our families had been linked by my marriage to her son. In writing my letter, I discovered that I had been so stressed by our relationship because I wasn't open to mothering and mother-wisdom of the kind that we receive from the more seasoned members of the female community. I don't know why this was. Perhaps it was because my own wound from losing my mother so young had not yet healed, some thirty-plus years later.

I read my letter over and over, and as I did, it occurred to me that I was not alone. As females, we have a way of nurturing others, usually children and men, but we are often reluctant to nurture and share with each other. As young women, we are often mean girls (or the victims of them). We might make a few close friends as young adults, but throughout our lives, many of us are very slow to let new women in. Rather than embrace each other, we push away. We argue with and resent our mothers, and more often than not, fall prey to the idea that our mothers-in-law and stepmothers, all "outside women," are evil rather than a source of support or knowledge. As we do so, we miss our lessons until finally we only see them in hindsight.

I invited other women to write a letter to a mother in their lives, someone who guided them when they didn't want to be guided and perhaps someone they'd never thanked. In the letter, they were to tell them what they wanted them to know. The recipient of the letter needn't be alive or biologically related, just someone to whom they had things to say to but lacked courage or foresight to be able to say those things, a thank you. Many of the writers I asked to participate agreed to do so right away. What I hadn't counted on though were those authors that were my friends who would refuse to participate. They had no issue with the concept. Instead, their reluctance was based on where they were in their own personal journeys with the mother figures in their lives. Some were not able to say anything positive so chose to say nothing. Others had no idea what they would say or they hadn't worked through their feelings about that mother-daughter relationship yet and they feared the experience would be too painful for them. There are emotional wounds that only another woman can inflict on you, and theirs had not yet begun to crust over. I received many calls and notes from those who did choose to participate, often filled with apprehension and tears. This task I was asking of them was harder than any of us had imagined, yet those who got through it reported experiencing a catharsis they had never counted on. The relationship that was closest to us proved to be the hardest to be honest about and the hardest to resolve. Writing these letters, love letters to our mothers, forced us to let go of the anger that had hung around our necks for years and let it float away from us. We had to give the bad memories to the universe and embrace the good and how that had shaped us into adulthood.

While I read the submissions, my love and respect for these women grew exponentially. I'd asked them to participate because I respected them and where they were in their craft and professional lives. I challenged them to look beyond the ordinary and find something positive in their relationship with their mothers. This proved to be harder for some than others, but once I was given a glimpse of their journeys and the women that had helped to shape them, they were all much bigger in my eyes. This process was like therapy for many of us, and as we navigated the murkiness of our childhoods, our paths through our womanhoods became that much clearer.

Charlenne T. Greer died May 31, 2012. Cigarettes killed her. She was not my mother or even related by blood. Still, I am thankful for her lessons.

Nina

A Letter to My Once Mother-in-Law
Nina Foxx

Charlenne,

The doctors say that it won't be long now. Your son just called and told me. I have to say that I didn't expect to be sucked down the long tunnel of dread, and I certainly didn't expect the tears. I haven't spoken to you in a month or so. That's mainly my fault. Since I split with your son, I don't call as much. I think it may have been a little uncomfortable for you, too, because you don't call me either, not like at first.

As young women, we are often told what type of relationship to expect with a mother-in-law, and unfortunately, we often believe it. That's where we started, in that place that every mother-in-law-daughter-in-law dyad is supposed to begin, midway between disdain and respect and halfway to fear.

Over time, we both figured that each was going to stick around awhile, so we had to get past the paper cuts and passive-aggressive behaviors that we inflicted on each other regularly. You would always be his mother and I would always be the mother of his children. No matter what we did or wished, our families would be linked forever. We learned that no matter what our differences were, there were some ways that we were alike, whether we liked it or not, and that there were some lessons that each of us had for one another.

We lived together for a brief time, and you told me things I knew you hadn't told anyone else, not even your own daughters, and you saw right through my designer-clad tough façade enough to call me out when I was hurting and break it down for me when I let injustice pass. Some of the things you said were not encased in pretty words to soften the blow, but that doesn't mean they weren't the truth. I had to learn that you had been where I was just starting to go. Time had taught you how to carry a burden with dignity, a lesson you were trying to pass on to me whether I wanted it or not.

I bitched, but you taught me a lot of things, and for this, I want to thank you. Some of the lessons were small. Although I acted like I was appalled, I know that you can use lipstick as blush in a bind. People used to do it all the time and just because new stuff hit the market, it doesn't make that untrue or even bad. Thank you. And it's true that it's cheaper to take my lazy ass to the post office to mail packages rather than go to the local shipping store. Thank you. Tuesday Morning does sell the BEST high-thread-count sheets at the cheapest prices. I will have sweet dreams many nights because of you. Thank you. I admit that Crisco works on baby eczema. You told me years before I read it in a fancy parenting magazine. Thank you.

Thank you for being the kind of grandmother that you were for my children. I had to learn to let you live in the space where you were comfortable. Thank you for baking a trillion dozen cookies with the girls even though I objected. I said that my kids couldn't have sugar and your lips said okay, but you were already firing up the oven. I know now that those early cookie lessons were also lessons in togetherness as well as lessons in math. Your love of the cookie-calculus will be carried on in your granddaughter, and I will make sure that she doesn't forget the real sugar (not Splenda) and knows what salted butter does to a cookie recipe.

You told me stories of your youth, and I acted embarrassed, but those were things I needed to know. You pushed me to be a better mother to my kids, to think outside convention and to demand respect from myself and from the men in my life, your son included. You reminded me that degrees don't make you smarter, just more educated, and that sometimes, plain old wisdom and not a text-book will get me to where I need to be.

I thought that when I broke up with your son, I was breaking up with you, too, but you didn't believe that. You didn't lose my number and didn't even change how you acted towards me and reminded me that my children were still your grandchildren and I was still your daughter, whether I wanted to be or not. Mothering doesn't always come from the person who is biologically your mother, and not everyone's mothering is the same, but that doesn't make it bad or not valuable. You urged me to keep my kids first and after you grilled me about what I wanted, you let me know that you were even woman enough to welcome whomever I let into my life next, into yours, too. If they made me happy, you would allow it.

I'm not sure when you'll go. The doctors don't know everything. Theirs is not the master plan. You were always strong-willed and definitely lived your life your way. You told me that many times, so I suppose you will go when you get good and ready. Good for you. The joke's on them, isn't it? You made me a promise a few years ago that you would let me know where you landed, and I know you will stick to that. I always have appreciated your stick-to-itive-ness, and I know this time won't be any different. I will welcome your message, and won't be afraid. Your presence in life challenged me to be a better me, so I can't imagine that your presence in death will be any different.

Thank you, Charlenne, for being a part of my village of women. I didn't expect to love you. I know now that the people who love you don't always have to make you comfortable. Sometimes, it is their job to make you examine yourself and your truths and shake things up, helping you to divine your path. You helped me to divine mine. I'm honored to have shared almost twenty years of your life.

Nina

Nina Foxx is an award-winning filmmaker, playwright and novelist. She writes as both Nina Foxx and Cynnamon Foster and has authored eight novels, contributed to several anthologies and co-authored a text on writing. Nina and her younger brother were raised by a single father in New York City.

Missing Mom
Carmen Green

There are days when I look for my mother and need her with a childlike desire that belies my forty-nine years. She's been gone for nearly six years, and it's her voice that I miss the most. It's her laugh that used to slide down me like warm chocolate milk. Her eyes were all knowing, and her pockets were endless with a wealth of tissue, warm, quick hands that smelled of sewing machine oil and cigarettes, and hugs that felt like so many yesterdays all rolled into one.

How can I still miss her so much? The loneliness without her defines a part of my life. Nobody and nothing can replace her.

Nobody "got" me like Mom.

You see, I'm different. I always have been. I stare off into vacant places and see imaginary things. I have secret smiles and gentle ways. The high days are high and the low days are low, but Mom understood them all. She knew I was special. I was just Carm.

At twenty-two, I told her I wanted to become a writer and she smiled that big bright toothy smile, *my own smile*, and said, "Carm, you go, girl!"

Buoyed by her ebullient laugh, laced by Kool cigarettes and coffee, I rode the wave of her glee into New York, publishing seven consecutive books in two years. Every success was a "You go, girl!" Her words were my rowboat, her confidence, my paddles during the mighty storm of my divorce. She was my champion, as tiny as she was. I became strong because of her. I became a woman to make her proud.

When she got sick, I would drape her in great big sweaters. "Mommy, where are you in there?" I would ask, and she would laugh so big.

I tried to help her, but she was tiny and so tough, none of us could break through her stubbornness. I needed her with a boundless wanting that was endless; I'd lost it all.

Love. My family, my home, and all of what I'd known. And I was losing her. I asked God, "How can you break my heart so badly?"

He answered me. She stroked my hair. "I'm going to be fine. It is well."

She'd already told me when it was time, it was time. She told me not to bring her back.

"*Yes, ma'am.*" As the oldest girl, I was the responsible one to follow her rules. To obey her laws. "It is well, Mom."

In that room, I stayed with her, told her unconscious mind the arrival time of each of her children. I blessed her. I gave her safe passage. I told her I would follow her wishes. I held her hand. I kissed her. I blessed her. I told her the time. I gave her safe passage. I kissed her. I told her I would follow her wishes. Over and over again until every one of my siblings, her children, arrived in town and came to the hospital.

And then I told them what she'd said so long ago.

We all cried, and I thought they might hate me just a little. But we couldn't bring her back.

She waited for me to leave the hospital, and then she crossed the mighty river Jordan. She knew I would be the first one begging to bring her back.

Dear Mom,

So much has happened since you've been gone. Life has been no crystal stair, but each step I build of brick and mortar, I seal with sweat and tears. They hold. Just like you showed me. The kids are adults and you'd be proud. College graduates, just as we'd talked about so long ago. My dreams for them are slowly coming true.

I still dream. Of the old house on Humboldt Parkway, of us planting tulips, laughing as we sat on the front steps, watching the cars go by, wondering where everyone was going. Now I know. Everywhere and nowhere. I wish I was back there so I could tell you about my day.

I'm trying to keep Dad here with us. He's fighting, trying to join you. He's as scared of me as he was of you. Secretly, I'm pleased, because he's easier to manage. The Mother's Day after you'd passed, he told me he saw you on the porch of the house, and you told him to take care of your flowers. I was uneasy. Dad believed in ghosts? And you were outside in your peignoir?

Naturally, Dad, being who he is, cursed at you and you told him to take care of your flowers and make sure nothing happened to them. Apparently you scared him so badly, he got Mr. Percy to cut the grass the following week, paying him two dollars. Well, why entrust me with this information? Why not one of the others? You had six kids. Why me? Because I was the weird one. I saw things. I could invent stories out of movements, tales out of thin air.

I could interpret what the ghost of my mother was doing on the porch.

I thought about your appearance until Grandma died three months after you. The family was devastated. We met at Bryant's after the funeral and Dad came to Baltimore. He sat next to me on the back porch under the tall pine tree. I asked him, "Have you seen Mom lately?" He told me he saw you every day.

Scared as I was, I wanted to know if you two had been chatting. He said you told him to "Watch out for your fucking flowers."

Now, Dad being Dad, I knew something was up. "Did Mom say 'fucking'?"

"No, I added that. But you get the picture."

I repeated to him, "She said 'watch out'?"

His lips jutted out. "That's right, and dammit, I never ran over her fucking flowers and she don't need to be bossing me around! I know how to cut grass!"

It hit me in the head like a ton of, well, pine cones. "Dad," I said, "it's a metaphor."

"A meta what?"

"A metaphor? A phrase that means something else. Mom wants you to take care of us. Her kids. We're her flowers."

My father looked out over the backyard at all of his children and their children and the tiny great-grandchild that my mother had nurtured, while he'd lingered on the periphery of our lives. He saw the awesomeness of what she'd done. What God had done.

"She coulda just said that," he mumbled.

"Give her a break, Dad. She's a ghost."

He looked at me with different eyes. "Mildred," he said, "don't you worry. I'll take care of your flowers."

I understood. I looked just like her. I took his hand as the wind lifted and the minty odor of sewing machine oil drifted by.

"Hello, Mom," I whispered.

A tear ran down my dad's face. We just enjoyed the day.

Carmen Green was born in Buffalo, N.Y., and had plans to study law before becoming a published author. While raising her three children, she wrote her first book on legal pads, before selling her first novel in 1993. Since that time she has sold forty-two novels and novellas, had one book, Commitments, *made into a TV movie, written and produced a play,* Who Decides? *in 2010, and written a short film* After Thriller *in 2013.*

Mamaji
Elisheba Haaq-Stevens

My mother died when I was three and for much of my life I thought this event had little or no real impact on me. I had not known her, and so I assumed that she had very little to do with what I would become.

As I grew older, I realized how wrong I was. I had tried for most of my life to pretend that my family was much like everyone else's. Everyone I knew had two parents and yes, sometimes they didn't get along with their parents, but in the end their parents loved them and would do anything for them. I tried to pretend that I, too, had parents like that. By the time I began high school, I could no longer pretend and I had to face what the loss of my mother meant. The realization was a painful one, because I had to admit to myself that perhaps the woman whom I called mother really didn't love me and that my father had also lost his love for me.

When I married, I often wished for a mother—my friends had mothers who called, visited, babysat their children, came over for coffee, shopped and laughed with them. I had a mother figure, who by this time had become more of an older friend and remained standoffish and uninvolved in my life.

I have written many letters and journal entries to my mother, to God, to anyone who was listening, hoping, wishing and imploring for answers. I didn't really find any, but I did find the courage to forgive and to love the family and friends I had. I know now that my mother had much to teach me, and she taught me the most important lessons I would ever have to learn.

I have written her many times over the years. This is a compilation of those letters.

Mamaji – Respected Mother
Nani – Maternal Grandmother
Nana – Maternal Grandfather
Masi – Maternal Aunt
Mammoo – Maternal Uncle
Purani – Previous or other

Dear Mamaji,

I still remember the last day I saw you. People (mostly the older kids) tell me there's no way I could remember the night you died. But I do, even though I was only three. The clear red flashing lights of the ambulance lit up the foyer where I was playing with Hannah. They carried you out on the stretcher and you reached out your hand, with a Band-Aid on your index finger, to us as you passed. It was your final goodbye to me, but I didn't know it. You looked tired and pale, I suppose the cancer had taken full hold of your body and the pain had worn you out. I remember when they told us you had died. Hannah and I pushed toy trucks up and down the green carpeting with the pattern cut into the pile. I heard someone say above my head, "Poor girls, they don't even know what happened." But I did know. I knew that my life would never be the same again.

There's so much you don't know about what happened after that night. Even though you asked Papa not to get married again, he did. I guess that was sort of selfish of you to ask that. After all he was only forty-five and he had seven kids to take care of. Now that

I'm a full-grown woman, I understand how you must have not wanted anyone else to have the man who was your one and only love. How I wish he had listened to you, because you were right.

Maybe it was because the Minnesota Child and Family Services threatened to remove David, Hannah and me and find homes for us. Maybe it was because he was lonely and couldn't get over losing the woman he had loved for so long. Maybe he was tired of taking care of all of us on his own. Maybe he just wanted to get back to normal. Whatever it was, about year or so after you died, he got married again.

The wedding happened in India and unlike your marriage to Papa, it was an arranged marriage. But when they met each other, she fell in love. I can't blame her. He was so very handsome and tall, full of confidence and pride. I didn't have anything to say about the whole thing, and I suspect neither did any of the older kids. I guess it doesn't matter, because it happened anyway. The well-meaning church ladies were all so happy for us. "You're going to have a new mother!" Was it a betrayal on my part to be really happy about meeting my new mother? And now, knowing all that happened, I feel disloyal to you for loving her as my mother.

The night she came to us was a cold night. I watched her as she walked out of the gate at the Minneapolis/St. Paul airport. I was woken from my sleep to go and meet her, so it must have been in the early morning hours. All seven of us were dressed in our best. You would have been so proud to see us. We were a beautiful family, anxious and hopeful. I remember she wore high-heeled pumps and red lipstick. At that time all I wanted was a Barbie doll and to me she looked just like the one I wanted. She was beautiful, healthy, strong, and smiling. I instantly fell in love with my new Barbie doll mother.

But she didn't love me back. Not me, not Hannah, not David,

not Debbie, not Emmanuel, not Eb and not Miriam—none of us. Oh, I think she maybe liked me at first. I remember she used to hold me on her lap and stroke my hair. I was so happy because instead of tearing up those Mother's Day cards I made at Sunday School, I actually had a mother to give them to. For a while, things seemed to work okay. She had left a career as a surgeon in order to marry Papa. After she got settled, she worked now and then, taking calls for some of the vacationing surgeons. Papa decided the house you and he had rented was too small, and they bought a new house in a small farming town about twenty miles south of Minneapolis. But then she got sick—she developed chronic high blood pressure and once more I was stuck with a sick mother. Migraines, dizzy spells, tiredness, irritability—she had it all. And once more I had to be quiet all the time. Even to this day, I go ballistic when anyone tells me to be quiet. I know it wasn't your fault you had cancer, but something I remember about both of you, is that I never had a mother who wasn't sick.

What I hated the most about those days, is that you completely disappeared. We couldn't talk about you, or who you were or what we missed about you. We were forbidden to write to Nani or any of our Masis or Mammoos. You and your entire family just disappeared and were replaced by a new Nana and Nani and a whole slew of new Masis and Mammoos who all hated us. We had to call her Mama—right away on the very first day. Even the older ones who had known you and loved you for most of their lives. When we were occasionally allowed to mention you, we had to call you Purani Mama. I hated that, and I hate it even more now. But we didn't call her Mamaji. No one could make us do that.

Two years passed and after a few miscarriages, she finally had a son. It was at this very moment, that I felt her disdain and disregard for all of us become most intense. Instead of being the children she never had, we became an obstacle to what could be her perfect family. Looking back, with the added benefit of time, I can see her point of view. We were constant reminders of you and a life that Papa had before she ever came into the picture. But I never asked her to come and it wasn't my fault that you died. The moment her son was born, I became an orphan. I had already lost you, and when he was born, Papa forgot all of us as well.

Maybe you know this, but I'm not a fast learner, not when it came to understanding her. While each of the older kids learned the hard lesson that we were nothing but a nuisance or a hindrance, and got married or moved out, I still hoped, prayed, sacrificed, kowtowed, and lowered myself in an attempt to gain her love. Because, as you can guess, Mamaji, it wasn't just about *her* love. Her approval of me was tied to Papa's approval. And even worse, I had to cower and curry favor with a snotty little kid, because I knew if her son liked me, she might like me and hopefully Papa would do the same.

Where were you in all those dark days? Why didn't you send a lightning bolt from the sky and strike me dead, like I prayed so many, many times? You were sitting next to Jesus and you couldn't have talked to Him and said, "Look at what's happening to my children. Stop her. Stop him. Help them." I tried so hard to hate you, but I didn't even know you well enough to hate you. I just hated my life.

I hated the way I had been abandoned not only by you and by Papa, but then again and again in succession as Miriam, Eb, Emmanuel and Debbie all got married and left the last three of us to contend and fend for ourselves. I hated that the three of us had to eat and drink from dishes, cups and utensils that were set aside and washed with the "common" sponge, while she used another set of dishes for herself, her son and Papa. She washed these and used a sponge Hannah and I could not touch. I hated that she only used bleach to wash our clothes and added them to the wash machine with a branch she had taken from the yard. I was a leper in my own house. I hated that my sisters and I did all the hard, heavy labor, cleaning from the time we were little girls, while her son only knew how to make messes. I hated that I was forever labeled Disturbed and Jealous because I acted out Hansel and Gretel and put my baby doll in the cold oven. She was convinced that it was her son that I wanted to cook. I hated the sound her spoon made when she mock-scraped the bottom of the pan to prove there was no food left, but when her son wanted more, there was always plenty. I hated how we ate the gizzard, neck, heart and liver of the chicken and watched hungrily as her son leisurely bit into a meaty, juicy leg and thigh. I hated that they could never afford our dreams of bikes, soccer balls or maxi dresses, but miraculously, all her son's demands appeared when he wanted them. I hated that I never had time to study in high school, because I was so overwhelmed with chores and yard work. I hated that I was put into trade school instead of college, because then I would be able to contribute the maximum amount of money back to the household. I hated that when I voiced my wish to pursue journalism as a career, I was laughed at and against my will, forced to train as a nurse. I hated that all my income was demanded when I got a full time job—until the day I got married. She used to mark all our pay days on that dammed Bible verse calendar of hers. I hated that I had to work three jobs to pay for college, still not able to choose my major, but was not allowed to buy any books. I was making more money than most of the grown men in my neighborhood. I hated that I told her "I love you" and "I'm sorry" so many, many times— I wish I could take those words back. I hated that when I got married, she told me "I won't cry at the wedding, because I already cried last night." Who cries preemptively? Unless they were tears of relief.

Surprisingly, I learned important lessons from my Barbie doll mother. I learned that women can do anything, no matter our age or situation. I learned that the best way to deal with a bully is to keep quiet. I learned how to respect my elders, even when it's difficult. I learned how to be creative with almost nothing. I learned that I can manage without mother love and that affection and friendship are sometimes enough. I learned that family is not always what you are born into or what grows around you. Family is made out of love and can be destroyed from lack of it. I learned how to forgive and move forward with life. I learned to lean on God more than ever because I found that humans, even parents, can be fallible and absent.

Mamaji, I often wondered what life would have been with you. I know you were not perfect. Many times I have been told of your famous quick temper and your strong will. Maybe we would have had our own trials and tribulations, but they would have been ours— between you, my real mother, and me.

Sometimes when my friends complain about their mothers, I want to scream. I find myself losing control for no reason. One day at work, a colleague told me her mother was annoying her because she wanted to come over to see the baby, again and again. She was upset because her mother brought her so many meals that her freezer was now too full. Imagine her surprise as I lost my temper (did I get that from you?) and through my tears shouted at her to be thankful that she had a mother at all. How I wish you had been there when my first son was born. I sat alone in that apartment, my breasts leaking milk, the infected stitch on my episiotomy swollen to the size of a grapefruit. It was impossible for me to sit down, both my son and I crying, as I desperately wished I had you to tell me what to do next. I wondered how I had angered God so much that he had taken you from me.

We never knew each other. You didn't know the girl I was, the teenager I became or the woman I am today. For a long time I wondered if I even loved you, because I didn't know who you were. But I have learned to love you over the years. I love you for giving me life. I love you for giving me my wonderful brothers and sisters who have been my rock and foundation since you left us. I love you for teaching me that good friends are precious and worth any amount of sacrifice. I love you for forcing me to be strong, think independently and unselfishly. I love you for teaching me compassion and empathy for people who have tasted the bitterness of life. I love you, because knowing that you were a part of my life, no matter how short, gave me the courage to break the cycle and raise my children the way you would have raised me. I love you for shaping my life. It sounds wrong to say it, but if you hadn't died, I wouldn't be the woman I am today.

I think about you more and more as I get older. I wonder if you and your entire family are enjoying a party in heaven and having a great time. I don't visit your grave, even though it's only an hour from my house, because what's the point? I don't get the answers I want. I want to ask if you are proud of me and what your dreams were for me. How would you have guided me? Did you love me? In many ways, I'm still a little girl, waiting for you to love me.

Your loving daughter,

Elisheba

Elisheba Haqq-Stevens was born in Chandigarh, India and immigrated to Minnesota as a child. She has a MFA in Creative Writing from Fairleigh Dickinson University and writes for SheKnows.com, The Female Patient and New Jersey Monthly. Elisheba has been a practicing pediatric registered nurse for the past twenty-five years. She lives in New Jersey with her husband and two sons.

Marian of Memphis
Pamela Walker-Williams

Growing up in my mother's shadow was not always easy. She was perfect. She was a fashion model. She was tall, five-foot-ten, thin with a cute figure, poised and always dressed like a movie star. Her skin was flawless without a blemish to be found. She could shake a tail feather—do the Twist and the Mashed Potato. To top all that off, she could really burn. People came from all over to get a taste of her Creole dressing and her Memphis barbecued spaghetti. Those were some high stilettos to try to fill.

I idolized my mother. My dream was to be just like her. This dream was on track until I reached the ripe age of twelve when it became apparent that I wasn't getting any taller. I stopped growing at the towering height of five-feet-four and that same year my skin broke out with acne. My delusion to be just like my mother would never come to fruition. Fortunately there was no pity party allowed in our house. "Get over it," my mother said, "you need to concentrate on what you have to offer to the world." She required me to get an education, encouraged me to study dance and inspired me to make a difference. These actions molded me into the woman I am today.

In the back of my mind, I will always hear her saying:

"Pamela… Always do your best."

"You can do anything you put your mind to."

"Be a credit to your race."

"Some people you have to treat with a long-handled spoon."

"A woman never tells her age."

"Girl, I am the same number of years older than you today as I was the day you were born."

And of course her famous "Put some paprika on it!"

Lord, that woman puts paprika on everything, potato salad, deviled eggs and her Creole dressing. If you name it, she is going to paprika it. To her, nothing is complete until it is properly garnished with paprika. Honestly, I think she buys it by the case.

I am going to break my mother's rule and tell you that I am fifty-seven years old. I can see her rolling her eyes at me now. But at my age, I realized that I am blessed to have a mother who is so young at heart. She still dresses as sharp as a tack, never leaves home without her makeup, can do the Wobble and the Cupid Shuffle, and of course she still wears high-heel shoes, though now she carries ballet flats in her purse.

My mother goes to church every Sunday and visits and feeds the sick and shut-in. We always look forward to her annual visit, because she still brings one suitcase that is full of food that she has properly prepared, "paprika-ed," and frozen for her flight from Memphis to Houston by way of Atlanta. And yes, the TSA folks love her.

Sadly, most of my village mothers have left to join the ancestors. Each of them, in their own way, was a blessing to me. I honor them by sharing my mom, the matriarch of our family, with my sister-friends who sometimes need a mother's touch, a word of encouragement, a shoulder to cry on, or a quick culinary lesson.

Dear Mama,

Thank you. Thank you for being the greatest mother a child

could ever have. I loved growing up in th shadow of your stilettos.
You taught me by example, and I can never repay you for everything
you sacrificed for me and all you demonstrated to me, to let me
know *you cared—*

I smile as I remember
All the love you shared.
Always there to guide me
To let me know you cared.
You who taught me right from wrong
You who wiped my nose
You who kept me neat and clean
You who ironed my clothes.
You who showed me how to cook
(and even ate my food)
You who woke me up each day
And sent me off to school.
You who gave me "mother wit"
To ensure my common sense.
You who told me to brush my teeth
"And don't forget to rinse!"
You who told me to put God first
And follow all of His rules.
You who said always beware
Of educated fools.
You who taught me to sing
"I come to the garden alone"
And… "If I can help somebody
As I pass along."
You who played jacks with me
And taught me to jump rope.

You who told me always dream
And never give up hope.
You who told me sticks and stones
Not words could break my bones.
You who sent me to the world
But free to come back home.
Mama, all I am today
Or have aspired to be
Is all because you cared so much
And are so good to me.

Pamela Walker-Williams is a digital media specialist who has designed web sites for some of the country's top authors. She has developed eLearning courses for astronauts and flight controllers and is the owner of PageTurner.net and Stiletto Press Publishing. Pam was born in Chicago, but moved to Memphis, Tennessee at an early age. She currently resides in Texas with her husband, and once a year shares her mother with her girlfriends.

Family Matters Most
Berta Platas

This summer I rediscovered a photo of my mom, taken over fifty years ago, soon after her arrival in the U.S. from Cuba. Just twenty-five years old, she stands in front of a tiled fireplace in a small room, confident in an elegant wool sheath and heels, her long, dark hair swept up in a chignon. Her smile reveals nothing of the uncertainty she must have felt, far from the support of her close and loving family, surrounded by strangers whose language she didn't understand. She must have been worried about her two little girls and tried to keep her own fright hidden away.

Her life wasn't supposed to take a sudden shift toward exile. She was supposed to be buying a house with her handsome husband, and planning a large family, to take her daughters to spend long summer days at her father's beach house in Guanabo, just outside of Havana, where sugary sands and soft waves would lull us to sleep in the sun, and raucous family parties blasted music and laughter late into the night. She'd been continuing the piano lessons she'd started as a child, and she loved to make clothes for my sister and me using the expert sewing skills she'd learned from the nuns at a convent school.

My father, a journalist, didn't want to frighten his young wife with the news his sources brought to him. Castro had already taken over the government, and the more Dad heard, the more his hopes for a newly freed Cuba waned. Dad joined the resistance, as his brothers and my mother's brothers had done. One by one, his contacts fell, captured, until he felt that the newly declared Communists were getting too close to him. It was time to go.

Mom couldn't have been too surprised. Her own parents, business people who'd run commercial fisheries and truck fleets, had left in one of their fishing boats, sure that there would be no future for capitalists in Havana. My grandfather's boat gave him a business start in their new life.

Even after fifty years, I still don't know all the stories that surrounded the decision to go, and some of the stories I do know should not be retold. Even today, people who stayed behind could be hurt by their telling, or so I've been told all my life.

My father applied for our passports, and we prepared to leave the country—but departure was delayed for a year when I cut the photos out of our passport books. I was four, they were pretty, and I knew how to use scissors. As a first art project, it was a humdinger. It is the only time in my life that I was spanked. I still remember how the seat of my little swing in the garage felt against my tummy, and thinking how unfair it was that the swing I loved so much would be part of the punishment. I'm sure Dad didn't swat me very hard, but for years after, I was sure that I'd tried to kill my family. He probably told me as much with each smack on my backside.

A few years ago I told my mother about how badly I felt about the passport photo mutilation. She laughed and said that it had actually helped us. Even though it took another year for new passports to be made, and Dad had to call in every favor he could and bribe the local police, my scissors trick allowed them to re-create themselves. The old passports listed Dad as a journalist, Mom as a teacher. The new ones took advantage of a side business Dad ran with his older brother, a SAAB dealership. He was now listed as a used car salesman, and Mom as a homemaker, hiding their education. At the time, and for long after, Castro tried to keep every teacher, every doctor. My parents were happily given the boot.

Our suitcases were allowed to contain one outfit each and minimal toiletries. Children were allowed one toy each. No jewelry, no photos, no mementoes. Once you decided to leave, your house was inventoried by the local neighborhood Defense Committee, so my folks encouraged our family to visit us and sneak out the good stuff before my parents declared that they were leaving. Mom managed to keep her platinum and diamond wedding ring by rubbing soap on the back to dull the gems so that they looked fake. It was a risk. A woman in line to board the plane with us was pulled aside after a diamond necklace was found threaded through her bouffant hairdo. She didn't make the flight.

Once in Miami, Dad was whisked off by the feds to be debriefed about the missiles that had been seen by U.S. spy planes. I remember seeing one of those up close in Havana, while walking with my Dad and his brother to a coffee shop. As they swung me in the air by my hands and they talked in low tones, I demanded to stop to look at the parade. The street was practically blocked by big green trucks that were towing a huge rocket ship with a big red star on it. It wasn't a rocket ship at all, and my dad picked me up, told me sternly to be quiet, and then ensured my silence with the offer of a Coca-Cola.

Everything in Miami was strange to us. We were sent to live in a tiny second-floor apartment that was crawling with huge cockroaches. Mom must have been horrified. I know I was, but my parents tried to make it a game. When we'd arrive at the apartment, they'd make us wait in the hall, then suddenly turn the lights on so that we could laugh at the scurrying roaches.

The view from our apartment window was of the neon-bedecked pizza palace across the street. We'd never seen one before. We tasted the pizza, but couldn't stand the smell. Cuban cuisine doesn't include cheese dishes. The pizza pie smelled like vomit. It wasn't until we lived in New York that we grew to appreciate it. Meanwhile, Catholic Social Services soon approached my parents about sponsor families in other cities, and we left Miami. Given the choice of Los Angeles, Chicago, New York and Pittsburgh, Dad asked, "Where are there no other Spanish speakers?" He wanted to disappear into America. We ended up in a Polish neighborhood in Pittsburgh, surrounded by warm neighbors who knew what it was to have to leave everything behind and start over.

We moved from Pittsburgh to New York City to Charlotte and finally, Atlanta. Through it all I was a normal kid. Neither too good nor too bad. But puberty hit just as we moved to Charlotte, where life was slower, and safer, and my parents gave us the freedom that the frightening first years, and later, life in busy and dangerous Manhattan, wouldn't allow us to have earlier.

I went from regular kid to full-blown brat, and once as a teen, when I'd missed another curfew and got caught in a lie, my mother wished aloud that I someday have a child just like me. It sounded like a curse. And it came true.

My mother, strong, but nonjudgmental when I was going through my rebel phase, helped me just as much with my children. After my father died, she quickly dismantled their house and moved to my sister's house in another state. My sister had moved away, my father had passed on, and then Mom moved—I have to admit, I felt orphaned. But after being batted from place to place for years, she deserved to have a choice.

It occurred to me that I'd taken her for granted all the years that she helped me raise my children. A simple thank-you is not enough. Much was made of my dad after he passed away, and deservedly so, but I don't want to wait for an obituary to recognize my mom for the hero she's been to our family, and to me.

Dearest Mami,

Having a daughter is a blessing and a curse. When I gave birth to a little girl after my three boys, I was thrilled, although you warned me that girls were harder to raise. You reminded me of my own teen years and how I had gone from model child to hair-raising rebel.

It was true. When I hit high school, I was wild for independence— literally—and fought every rule, every curfew. When you found my fake ID and said that you hoped I'd one day have a daughter just like me, I thought there was nothing wrong with that. Yikes. You win. I now have a lovely child who questions every request, defies rules, and is a total slob. She'll soon be nineteen, and is maturing *very* gradually, as her three brothers did before her. I'm caught between exasperation and understanding, because I know what it's like to be in her Doc Martens. On the other hand, I also understand that some of my defiant, youthful choices made my life harder for me, and I want to spare her the consequences.

Nowadays your advice is always welcome, and it's more about how to cope with the kid down the hall, because she certainly isn't heeding any of our wise counsel. The other day I actually told her that I hoped one day she'd have a daughter just like her. I almost laughed as the words came out of my mouth.

In the mid '70s, when we moved to Atlanta where Dad was to be a Spanish professor at Morris Brown College, you must have thought that the tough times were over. You'd managed to move your position in mutual funds for one of the big New York brokerage firms to Charlotte, then Atlanta, and had applied to work as an elementary school teacher in Fulton County.

Life had been tough for so long. In Pittsburgh, though you were trained as a teacher, you'd gotten factory work because you didn't speak English, and had to rely on me, a ten-year-old, to translate on the phone for you. In Manhattan, where we all lived in a tiny apartment, you had to trust that your preteen daughters could safely walk to school and back, and stay alone in the apartment until you or Dad arrived home. You and Dad worked long hours and also went to college to recertify the degrees you'd gotten in Cuba, where Castro's government wouldn't release or verify any documents that would make life easier for exiles.

Finally, in Atlanta, you were in a good place. A destination where prosperity wasn't guaranteed, but at least was more likely. And it worked out that way. You and Dad bought a home, you established a career as an educator, got a master's degree, and married off both daughters.

Last winter I saw a photo of you that I'd never seen before. You were freshly arrived in Pittsburgh, and stood in the parlor of our rented rooms, smiling and elegant in an expertly fitted dress that you'd made yourself using couture skills learned in Cuban schools where you were prepared for a life very different from the one you ended up with.

You stand tall and beautiful in the photo, slender but curvy, with huge brown eyes and a wide, confident smile. You were only twenty-five years old, and you had fled your country with your husband and two young daughters. You hadn't seen your parents in two years, and many of your relatives and friends were in danger back home. You were among strangers in Pittsburgh, a cold, alien city. Did you think that you'd never see Cuba again?

You seemed so in charge. If you were afraid, you hid it from Laura and me. I remember being frightened at having to make phone calls for you or Dad, because you didn't speak English, but you met with my teachers, took me to the doctor—all the normal things that other mothers did in our blue-collar Pittsburgh neighborhood.

That strength and confidence are a part of me. If I didn't inherit those attributes from you, then I borrowed them and forgot to return them, so long ago that they're mine now. I love how you got your first office job. You had been working in a fiberglass curtain factory, coming home itchy after long hours at a commercial sewing machine. One day, at Gimbels department store, you saw a bookkeeper whose boss stood over her, angry about a ledger that sat on the glass counter in front of them. You, the math whiz, reached out and ran a finger down the column, doing the numbers in your head, and produced the correct answer. They immediately offered you a bookkeeping job, with better hours and easier work. You spoke no English, but who needs English to do math? Back then, there were no anti-immigration movements, and the Spanish-speakers were in Texas border towns, in New York City, Los Angeles, and just beginning to pour into Miami from Cuba. With no English classes, you learned through total immersion.

Later, when you had made teaching your career, you returned to college at night to get your master's degree. As I was writing this it occurred to me that I'd never asked you how you did it. I only assumed that if it had to be done, so be it.

It's the way I've run my entire adult life. Work full time, go to school, write novels and mind the kids. Sure, I can do it. Mom did, and with a smile and no complaints. You've done that all the years I've known you.

When I married, you rejoiced in my happiness and planned the wedding. Twenty years later, when the marriage fell apart, you were there for me, with comforting words and help settling into a new place. You gave advice when I asked for it, without judgment. I thanked you, but I don't think I could ever show you how grateful I am for your help and guidance.

You were present at the birth of each of my children, and with my youngest son, you were actually in the room the entire time, because the medical team forgot to make you leave. I looked over, deep in epidural la-la land, and saw you with your fists against your mouth, eyes wide, both excited and horrified. I knew you understood what I was going through, and that the moment meant as much for you as it did for me. As John entered the world, he saw you, right after he saw me and his father.

It was so important to have you close by as they grew up. They think so, too, and often call you for advice before they call me, especially for travel tips, since you've been to so many places, both with Dad and with your sister and nieces. You are totally the matriarch of this clan.

At the clothes store, when I check seams for good construction, I use the sewing knowledge you taught me in an attempt to teach me patience. When Nora Roberts has a new book out, I know you'll be hunting it down, and that you'll be the first of your friends to read it. Your library card probably smokes from overuse, just like mine. Your love of reading is infectious, and your keen eye has made my books better.

Every family should have a version of you. The one who calls everyone, keeps track of birthdays and encourages family to get together. When an aunt has surgery, a cousin announces a pregnancy, or a family friend finishes chemo, the news travels the family circuit through you.

Last year, when it became clear that Dad was not long for this world and you were exhausted from caring for him twenty-four hours a day, you still pulled him from the nursing home where the hospital sent him after they decided there was nothing else they could do for him. His heart was failing, but the nursing home confused and frightened him, and because he didn't complain, and you were always there to help him, the staff gave other patients priority. You brought him back to spend his last days at home.

Leaving him at the nursing home had been a heartbreaking decision, but bringing him home for hospice care nearly killed you, especially the physical exertion. Dad was skinny, but strong. The hospice nurses came by daily, and I helped when I could, but you were with him all night, and had to run interference when he became outraged at the invasion of privacy when the nurses bathed him. He wanted you to do everything. It was heartbreaking, both to see him deteriorate and to see you reeling from exhaustion and fright.

He died in your arms, surrounded by family.

You chose the harder path, but the easier one for Dad. That is true love. You showed us that family comes first, and that we make sacrifices for those we love. We'll move that lesson forward to coming generations, thanks to you.

I know Dad's passing still hurts, but I can see that you're applying your energies to your own life now, to your own dreams, and making plans for your future. I'm so proud of you, Mami, and so grateful for all you've done for us. Now you'll do what's most important to you.

Live big, Mom. You've proved you can do anything.

Berta

Berta Platas writes Latina women's fiction for St. Martin's Press and coauthors the popular young adult urban fantasy series The Faire Folk Saga *as Gillian Summers with longtime friend Michelle Roper. Her short stories and novellas have appeared in several anthologies. She lives in Atlanta with her husband and one daughter.*

Taming the Beast
Shia Shabazz Smith

Dear Beverly,

I love you, but...

Even the idea of writing this letter is a challenge for me. The mother/daughter thing that we have has been romanticized fantasy at its best, nightmarish at its worst. Like...

September 30, 2005. You were living with me in Austin, post Katrina and I was deeply delighted that life put us in that space for healing and closure. Before the midnight ringing in of my October 1st birthday, sometime between basting turkey meatballs and face paint, you jested for the last time. "Man! You'd better be glad your dad didn't believe in abortions!"

"Please don't ever say that again. It hurts my feelings," I interrupted. And, for the umpteenth time, I would go on to promise never again to allow you to celebrate my life with me. And, once again, I meant it. You pouted, but we pushed through that moment and I managed to have a beautiful celebration. The weight of the comment always found me, though. Though I always knew it would come, it also always felt like a sucker punch. It's something I never got used to.

Being the child your mother wanted to abort and the sister your nearly Irish-older-twin never wanted is, what the screenwriter in me knows to be, the beginnings of a great character arc. The daughter, however, could never make sense of it. A sensitive child, when I grew up to give birth to my first child, a daughter, your behavior seemed more and more unfathomable. From the moment she was born, I could never imagine not wanting her, not learning from her, and most of all, not wanting to be better because of her. No matter how lovable I felt, the choices you made seemed to have little, if any, regard for me as your child; as my example, as my protector, as my mother.

> Infanticide
> As it turns out,
> if your mother
> tells you she loves you
> then offers you as tribute,
> sends you into the den
> where The Lion waits
> rubs paws, laps chops,
> it does not mean
> she doesn't love you.
> It just means she loves him
> more.

That birthday in 2005 was the last time I feel like I really saw you; the debutante who married, mothered and divorced my father before I was old enough to utter my own name. The you that played dead long enough to elicit my childhood panic and tears. The you who taught me to tenderize, season and broil a steak and concoct the perfect root beer float. The you whose quick wit and work registered me at Tuskegee in record time. The you who created country ditties and lullabies.

The you I had grown up to, like it or not, accept as dynamically contradicting and painfully flawed. In your presence, I can feel both abandoned and embraced within a matter of heartbeats. I keep thinking there must be some great epiphany I am meant to come to about parent-child relationships, mothers and their daughters, imperfection. And every time I feel like I've finally gotten some kind of handle on it, finally unraveled the yarn of our relationship or gotten closer to what any of this means, some great catastrophic wind wraps the strings tighter, makes the knots more intricate.

> ...she is a shadow of herself
> perhaps she left decidedly
> her last intentional move
> perhaps she was kidnapped
> taken hostage somewhere
> between intoxicants and Katrina
> somewhere caught in the ruse
> scams and scandal, of who she once was
> and the habits that now choose her...
> *(from "Gone," 2012)*

Dementia is a beast. It is the band of termites chomping away the rickety wooden bridge that keeps the daughter in me from accessing the mother in you. If I had known then what I found out the day you were abandoned and delivered into my care, I would have written this letter long before now when I might have had a shot at leaving at least a portion of this in your person.

Regardless, I want to say...

Thank you, Mom, for choosing to have me. I don't say that lightly because without that choice, above all, there would be no me and subsequently, no "sweetie girl," no "sweet boy," no "Wonkin-pun-kin," no realization of unconditional love. Instead, there would have been the choice of clinic and sterile surgical tools, laughing gas and vacuum, recovery and only one child to speak of on that one child's first birthday. But, be it the urging of my father or the failure of attempts to end the pregnancy, it was still your body and I thank you for bringing me into the world.

Now, more than ever, I must thank your mother, Clarina "Nana" Williams, for bringing you into the world and mothering me when you could not. Her insistence that I am, and always have been, beautiful inside and out, is an elixir these days, long after the unimaginables and the unfathomables. I may not have heard or believed it growing up; but, the sentiment stuck with me into adulthood, when the chronic pains of unhealed childhood wounds hurt most. Even further, as I journey daily with children who have "special needs," I encourage them to believe the same of themselves. I know firsthand that it heals the broken parts when said in repetition. It is a meditation when the world feels too much, or when the opposite feels overwhelmingly true. (Thank you, Nana.)

The hard reality, Mah, is that you broke my heart before any man could, and I spent most of my early life chasing maternal love in the shadows of women who were too busy to notice. By the time I was sent to live with my father, who had saved my life for the second time, I was more than the women in his life could, or wanted to, handle. The women he went on to marry—the ones I hated out of youth and solidarity to you—taught me what not to tolerate and how to empower and love myself (thank you, Mama, "Meelah") and how to run a household with maternal purpose and intention (thank you, Maryam.)

By the time I entered relationships, I was already a blues song stroking the myth that I could never be enough for anyone's love, in the same ways I think you believed it about yourself.

But we are both worthy, Mah.

As a mother of three, I get it now. Trying to navigate the often tumultuous waters of relationships and multitudinous matters of adulthood is hard. And on top of it all, you've got kids who only know how to need from you.

I asked my mother
What there was to love
About a middle child...
...My head in her lap
Mother traced love
Around my pleading face
Like a sonnet in Braille
Cupped my face in her hands
Whispered softly,
"Everything."

There are moments etched in my memory that made me feel like ONLY you loved me. Like every touch was an apology, every word a prayer. Many of those moments feel like the beginnings and endings of chapters in my life, which is lucky for me because the pain-filled middle pages are blurred with tear stains, rippled out or forgotten in the way that survivors train themselves to forget things.

It seems logical that the story of my early years also planted the seeds of your undoing. Having had my own first, failed marriage, I understand how the pains of it break your heart in unrecoverable ways. I only wish, when you looked into my eyes as a child, I was whole enough to have saved your life like my children did mine. Maybe in that way, you saved my life then so that I could save yours now.

 The torrents of pity and anger and hostility I've felt toward you, toward the disease, toward this folded hand only remained as the shrapnel of memory and flesh by the time you landed at my doorstep, abandoned and alone. Laughing inappropriately and wondering how we'd both gotten so old and stayed so cute, you are now the concentrated you; full shot, no chaser. I don't think I really knew who I was until you showed up requiring so much of me.

> *when I die, I'm gonna leave*
> *Everything to you...*
> my mother's incessant
> promissory note
> for these days
> when i do Everything
> draw every bath
> spoon every meal
> change every soiled sheet.
> but there is Nothing to bequeath
> beyond stubby third toes on each foot
> a stinging self-deprecating wit, insatiable need
> and the possibility of forgetting

Everything.

Rearranging my life in the short term—new marriage and toddler included—felt nothing compared to the long haul ahead of you. I can't imagine what you feel like on even your best days but I am grateful your laughter enraptures you. Even on the cloudy days, you bring me clarity about what life is about and what gratitude means. You tell strangers you love them and dance whenever even the thought of music enters your mind. You, the debutante turned free-farter, have made me laugh at myself and realize that even if THIS is all there is, THIS is plenty.

Mom... I. Love. You. (period)

Shia

Shia Shabazz Smith is a Cave Canem Fellow, a member of The Austin Project: Experiments in the Jazz Aesthetic, and a teaching poet in UC Berkeley's Poetry for the People Program. An accomplished poet, performance artist, activist, and screenwriter, Shia lives in Oakland, California, where she enjoys walking Lake Merritt and eating tiramisu.

There is a Time
Gabrielle Cox

There comes a point in life when a child and a parent must separate. Or at least, that is what is supposed to happen. My mother lives by a slightly different ideology. Her thoughts are more like: "There comes a time in a child's life when they may want to leave. Don't let them. Put them in a choke hold if you have to." That might be a slight exaggeration. But this summer after I moved back home, it felt like my reality. My mom and I clashed. In a game of tug and war, I was working to establish my independence. My mom kept trying to reel me back in. As annoyed as I was, I failed to realize something, my mother was having a harder time than I was. My walking away added to the sorrow she faced from having to let me go. Her firstborn was entering the world of adulthood. As I started to venture down my own path, she was faced with a harsh realization: She couldn't keep me. As she went through this difficult time, I failed to provide something my mother needed greatly: respect and gratitude.

When I moved home the summer after graduating from college, I checked my freedom at the door. All of my liberties, left behind in Boulder, Colorado. My loving parents welcomed me with open arms, some added regulations and a nice little list of everyday chores and responsibilities. I felt like I didn't have a choice, but to comply with their rules. I needed my parents, mainly for financial support. I wasn't working that summer. It wasn't for lack of effort.

No one was hiring. And all of a sudden, I was depending on my parents for things I had supplied for myself over the last two years. I needed help with everything from tuition to gas money. The last two years of college, I handled my rent, tuition, books and just about everything else. My unfortunate state left me in a bind; I was at my mother's disposal. I started babysitting, running errands and cleaning, to my dissatisfaction.

Added chores had me feeling like I had shifted back in time. Some new rules from my parents threw me into another dimension. Like a curfew. That summer, they always wanted me home before midnight. It was a huge detour from my college days. They expected me to be the little girl who didn't have a car, who needed permission to hang out with friends. There were days that, I'd get up in the mornings to find my parents gone and my younger brothers looking at me, hungry. "Gab, what's for breakfast?" It was suddenly clear. In my mom's eyes, the live-in babysitter had returned. I soon felt that no amount of griping, complaining or whining could remind her that I wasn't a little girl anymore.

As annoyed as I was, I conceded to their rules, even though I felt like a kid, and in many aspects, I was treated like a kid. As hard as it was for me, it pained my mother. Day after day I witnessed the deep hurt in her eyes as she began to realize the inevitable; I was slipping away. So were two of my brothers. Aaron was working his first job and gearing up for his senior year of high school. Brandon was just wrapping up his first year of college and busy with three jobs. We were venturing out, and didn't bother being discreet about it, either. All my days were spent with my boyfriend as I relished in my new relationship. My brother, Brandon, was the same. His long-distance girlfriend was back from college, and he couldn't be happier. "I have plans," was our slogan that summer. Then, a car accident changed things.

My family lives in Monument, Colorado. It's beautiful, quiet, secluded and located just off of an extremely dangerous two-lane road. My brother, driving home late one night, fell asleep. He was overcome with fatigue from working his three jobs and spending time with his girlfriend. His eyes closed for a few seconds. It was just enough time for him to fly off the road. He flipped our Land Rover that night. The front of the car where he and Aaron were sitting was smashed in. After this near tragic accident that almost claimed two of my brothers' lives, everything changed.

The need to protect us sent my mom into overdrive. They didn't want us driving at night any more, hence the curfew. And almost the thought of losing my brothers had her holding on even tighter. When we went out at night, my mom didn't sleep until we walked in the door. Following the accident, my parents decided to hold a family meeting. I dreaded the idea of it, thinking it was only another chance to add some more rules to an already growing list. I was so wrong.

My mom sat in front of us, with a sad and pained expression. For the next half-hour, she would speak about how hard of a time she was having letting go. "Your dad and I are entering into a new stage of parenthood," she explained, "We're trying to figure it out." That meeting was hard for her; she even explained her tendency to hold on to us, so she would have to let go. I was hit with a realization; no annoyance or frustration compared to her ache. I spent the summer complaining about her expectations of me. That was the wrong move. She wouldn't have me around for too much longer; with that, I should have done so much more. I had failed to my mother.

For the prior twenty-two years of my life, my mother had been selfless. She forsook her dreams and want of a career in the hope that she could help her children have the best life possible. I am the product of my mother's influence in my life. I know now that no amount of babysitting or cleaning can replace her sacrifices.

Dear Mom,

Here I am, twenty-two years old and a morning producer in one of the top news markets in the nation. I owe a great deal of this to you. That fact is something I'm just now realizing and it's long overdue.

When I was younger, my elementary teachers would have me write about my hero. I always wrote about Dad. Remember that? I know you do, because you bring it up from time to time. I saw Dad as this great person, rising from the dust of New York's ghetto and becoming a force in the military. You were just a housewife. At that age, I also paraded around our home declaring that I would never be a housewife. I didn't see cleaning in my future, I'd get a maid for that. Looking back, I know that must have hurt your feelings. It didn't matter how I may have insulted you. Your love for your children led you away from your dreams. I know that now.

You didn't plan on being a housewife. You didn't plan on being a support system for four rowdy boys and me. Not to mention the added stress and responsibility of being a pastor's wife. You've explained the reasoning behind your choice. Dad's job in the military kept him abroad and the family moving every two-and-a-half years. Your kids needed stability, and we'd get it by having you around.

Years later, your labor may have sometimes seemed to be in vain. We're spoiled. The boys more than me. I would like to stop and say that you and Dad sure knocked it out of the park when you had me. These days we depend on you for everything. Cooking, cleaning, homework, driving, mentoring all falls on your shoulder. Even when I was back in high school, I didn't do enough to help you bear your load. Instead of helping to alleviate your burdens, we just toss more responsibility on your shoulders. When the boys and I were younger, we copped the biggest attitude if you dared ask us to turn off the TV and fold clothes. Looking back, our treatment of you wasn't what it should have been. You were simply the fun-killer.

If you never hear this from anyone else, you'll hear it from me. You're more than what this family has made you out to be. We've diminished your role and the significance that it plays in our lives. I can't speak for Dad or the boys, but I know that sometimes I take you for granted. In many aspects, we all do. We know that you will be there, to run lunchboxes to school, visit sick church members in the hospital, help me pack and move. We need you more than we realize, even as I'm writing this letter, I'm realizing how much.

As a family, we perform better when you are around. Joshua improved his reading with your help and attention. Dad's cholesterol would be through the roof without you. There'd be no one to pick up Aaron when he frequently gets sick at school. Then there's me. I wouldn't have my drive or motivation without you.

No one is as hard on me as you. When my performance doesn't match my ability, you remind me, again and again. I can truthfully say that I am not my own worst critic. It hurts my feelings when you watch my resume reel and critique everything. It goes something like: "Gab, you look so pretty here, but in this other one, you look frazzled. And this one looks old-womanish." Thanks, Mom, and I mean that both sarcastically and sincerely. I don't come to you for comfort or pity. That's because you don't give it, even when I beg. You push me past my comfort zone and into my successes.

No amount of cleaning, vacuuming, babysitting could repay you. During my time spent at home, I should have done so much more to help you. But the good news is, I'm still here and so are you. I pray to God that we have many more years together. This time around I won't let you down. I won't fail to remind you have how special you are and how my life would be lacking without you.

Gabrielle Cox lives in Colorado and works as a morning producer for CBS4 in Denver, Colorado. Gabrielle graduated from the University of Colorado Boulder with a degree in Broadcast News.

Gloria
Gillian Hubbard

Last year, I asked my mother if I could take a photo of her hands for an art series I was working on. She asked, "Oh, why would you want a picture of my old, wrinkled, bumpy hands?" My response was "You look at them and see wrinkles and bumps. I see the beauty marks of other hands held, foreheads checked for fevers, diapers changed, wounds bandaged, meals cooked, sweaters knitted, and hundreds of babies delivered and other mothers comforted at St. Luke's when you were a nurse." She shyly smiled and found it a much nicer way to think about herself. That was a good day.

Dear Mom,

When my friend told me about a group of women writing letters to their mothers, I knew immediately that I would write one, because I marvel at you. Then I was afraid. I guess like a lot of mothers and daughters, getting to the point of marvel took a long time. I worried that I would hurt your feelings if I wrote truthfully about the years of loneliness, anger, confusion and pain that preceded the joy I now hear at the sound of your voice, and when I'm very fortunate, when I see your beautiful face, and receive a hug that I now understand only a mother can give.

I'm not a mother, so I talked with a dear friend with children about my fears and my strong desire to honor you for what to me, feels like a Herculean show of love from you that changed me, and our relationship. She warmly assured me that every mother wants to hear from her kids that she's done the right for them, and that I should quit overthinking it. I started writing. Right now, I'm not sure I'll show to you, ever. Maybe I'll change my mind.

As I write this you are nearly eight-five, I'm forty-seven, and we are closer than I'd dreamed we could have been. I couldn't ask for more, and this happened because about ten years ago, you gave me a miracle gift. Maybe others will find this an exaggeration; it's not like you gave me a kidney or something! But, I know we both remember how difficult it used to be.

Mom, you're a reserved person, and as you've recently said, you can't find the words, or have difficulty expressing how you feel. You've also accepted and said that you have trouble with depression. These qualities left me feeling alone, scared, and insecure when I was a kid. When I met people whose parents were more effusive and joyful, I was amazed that some families were like that. I felt cheated, unloved and very angry. I needed you to show me, in a way I could see and feel it, that you loved me. Of course I didn't know how to say it, or that what I was feeling was unworthy.

There were many, many, wonderful times, and countless moments when you were selfless for me. I recall with great warmth squeezing into a recliner with you, next to the fire, while we read books, watched movies, or had a nap. I remember the hundreds of long hikes with you through the woods, finding beautiful treasures on the spongy, fragrant forest floor. You took me to the library nearly every week, and eventually I read almost every kid's and young adult book there. I remember you staying up with me for hours, my head in your lap when I had earaches. I now know that you used the couple of hundred dollars that you inherited from your parents to buy us a pool; that you asked for a swing-set one year as your Mother's Day gift from my dad. I know you sacrificed nearly everything so I could have a new bike, pretty prom dresses, and a college education. I know you cleaned out a savings account so I could study abroad. I remember that when I was seven, you found me so beautiful in that green dress with the white Peter Pan collar that you put it on layaway because the extravagant twenty-dollar price was too much to pay all at once. You always told me, "I love you."

You are generous to others. You never had a garage sale or sold anything in the *Pennysaver*. When you didn't need things, you found someone who did and gave them a gift. You and Dad experienced the Great Depression, and struggled financially yourselves, yet you remembered that there were always people whose lives you could make a little easier. You delivered Meals On Wheels, and took care of the elderly neighbors. You drove them places and removed the snow from their driveways all winter. Being in upstate New York, that often meant being out in temperatures well below freezing more than once a day. There was a neighbor who was known for her surliness, and when she could no longer drive, you took her everywhere for years. My favorite thing was the handmade sweater you made for us when we were kids, the word "Hello" was knitted on the back. People commented on them, and over the years, just about every new baby in the neighborhood had your famous "Hello sweater." You made them for my friends' kids; people you'd never met. Even one for my friend in Israel, with the word knitted in Hebrew. You knew how much people appreciated them and kept knitting with arthritic hands; sometimes it took you months. You did this until you simply couldn't work the needles anymore. Yet, when I asked for a poncho a few years ago, not knowing how bad your arthritis had become and that you no longer knitted, you made it for me. I'll keep it forever.

Through all of these actions, you built in me a sense of adventure and creativity, an endlessly curious mind, an understanding of the importance of handling my finances with great care, and a generous heart. My life has been one big adventure, I'm fearless, I endlessly and joyfully learn and create. I'm financially secure, and never worry about how I'll care for myself. I have compassion and I give. These are the things I love the most about myself, and they are all gifts from you.

Yet, I couldn't see those things for decades. All I could take in was your criticism, stern look, and what felt like constant disapproval. I was stuck on times when, after spending hours getting ready for a special occasion, you looked at me and asked, "Do you have a plan for your hair?" All I could muster was a sarcastic comment that I knew you wouldn't understand; it would belittle you, "What do you want me to give you, a spreadsheet?" Incidents like when I drove four hours to your house, arranged for a U-Haul, drove you two hours to your sister's house, loaded the U-Haul with furniture, and drove you back to my brother's house. All of this because you wanted him to have the furniture, and he wouldn't go with you to get it. When I finally sat down after two long days of this, all you said was "I don't care for the color of those pants you're wearing." I threw another sarcastic response, "Well then, I won't get them for you for Christmas." I felt rage, pain, and bewilderment at those moments. I didn't have the words, the courage, or the ability to understand or express what I felt. All the negative, hurtful feelings kept growing.

Then that day about ten years ago, the miracle occurred. I was living in Brooklyn, and you asked me to drive you to a wedding in Virginia. I was happy to do it; really I was. Doing these things for you let me feel wanted, important, and loving. I knew you appreciated it, and I knew that asking for help was difficult for you. I pulled out my favorite dress, bought some new shoes, took two days off from work, rented a car, made the hotel reservations, and when I picked you up at Penn Station, you hugged me, touched my hair and said, "Huh, your hair looked so nice the last time I saw you." I swallowed it, and braced myself for the weekend. Dad had died about a year earlier, after you'd been with him for fifty-three years. You said it felt like an amputation. Imagining how that felt was impossible for me, but I knew it was excruciating. I had been working very hard at being gentle and looking past these things. We arrived at the hotel, after four hours of driving. I unpacked and realized I had forgotten to bring something. As I left for the store, you took out my dress and said it was wrinkled; you would iron it. I asked you not to; it was delicate and nobody would notice. When I returned, my dress was wrinkle-free and the fabric was ruined. I took out my shoes and your comment was "do you think it wise to wear those shoes?"

Now, you and I rarely argued. I was afraid to, and your reaction had always been walking away. But that night, I lost it. I raised my voice about the ruined dress, you never listening to me, treating me like an idiot who can't pick out her own shoes, and for saying it when we had ten minutes before we had to leave for the wedding, in a strange town—there was nothing I could do about it even if I wanted to. Even though I was terrified, you were the only parent I had. I would have felt orphaned if you weren't there. I told you that I could no longer have a relationship with you if you didn't stop poking at me and criticizing me. You ran into the bathroom and cried, saying that you don't know why you even try to do anything. I was blind with anger and outrage; we had a miserable time at the wedding; we couldn't even speak.

The next day, our world changed forever. After many painful hours, you put your arm around me and said, "I guess I just can't get used to you not needing me." Jaw dropping. All this time, I had thought you didn't like me, felt that I was incompetent, and that you were just plain mean-spirited toward me. "I need you, I will always need my mother. I never want you not to be with me; I just need you to let me be."

You responded, "I guess that's just how my mother always treated me."

"Did it feel good?" I asked.

"No."

That's all it took. It was like you flicked a switch, and you have never treated me like that again. I feel that kind of change is incredible under any circumstances, but to change immediately, at seventy-five after being together for a lifetime, is a miracle born of the purest love of a mother.

Now, at nearly eighty-five, your mind is faltering. Your short-term memory doesn't cooperate anymore, and you're easily confused. This is excruciating for all of us. I worry about you constantly, having picked you up off the floor twice, and last month needing to explain to you that your son no longer lived with you; he had his own house for sixteen years. You were upset when he didn't come home to sleep. I'd do anything to help you, to bring you fully back to us, but it's not possible. Instead, I embrace your innocence, increased openness to a wonderful array of emotions, and feeling deeply grateful for you. Especially for that day ten years ago when you changed my life in the most beautiful way.

Gillian

Gillian Hubbard is an artist and a psychologist. She earned a Ph.D. in Industrial Organizational Psychology in 1999 and worked in several Fortune 25 companies. Passionate about art, she took classes at the School of Visual Arts in New York City and at the Contemporary in Austin, Texas. She now works full time as an artist while doing management consulting on the side. Gillian lives in Austin and frequently returns to upstate New York where she visits her sweet and adoring mother.

Just Enough
Arlene L. Walker

I never once doubted that my mother loved me. Anyone looking could see that she did.

I knew it by the way she kept my brothers and sisters and me—all eight of us—close to her. Growing up, she rarely let us go down the street to play with neighborhood children; not even with our cousins on our dad's side who lived next door, and whose behavior she deemed questionable.

I knew it when I came home from school one day complaining, "Mama, Monique doesn't like me. She plays with everybody, except me." I folded my hands across my chest, and pouted my lips.

Mama stopped stirring her pot of pinto beans then and there (because she was always either cooking or cleaning, or catering to my dad), wiped her hands on her apron, and said, "Well, what's wrong with her?" The whole left side of her face curled into a quizzical expression that said: *She must be crazy if she doesn't want to play with someone as wonderful as you. She should go see a doctor for that, get some medicine for it.*

BAM! Just like that, I felt better. I felt so good, I laughed Monique off as unimportant. Even if Monique didn't like me, my mama did. I felt secure in my heart that my mother loved me. She didn't have to say it with words.

But I wanted her to. Badly.

When a child doesn't hear the words "I love you" from the one who is supposed to love them the most no matter what, it can affect the entire rest of their lives. They may become mentally scarred or emotionally impaired. Or maybe they grow up looking for love from whoever *will* say it, however wrong that person may be for them. Or maybe they continue the cycle by marrying some-one who never says it, either, and then they have kids who never get to hear the words. Or maybe they grow up with low self-esteem, thinking that they aren't quite good enough, that they are inade-quate somehow. Or maybe they learn to love themselves.

When your mother doesn't say the words "I love you," it's like eating her peach cobbler—you know, the cobbler that everyone looks forward to at Christmas—and not being able to taste its awesome sweetness. You saw her put the sugar in it, so you know it's there. You can smell its buttery goodness as you shove a spoon-ful of it toward your mouth. But when it hits your tongue, it tastes like something is missing. It doesn't quite hit the spot. It took you to the brink of satisfaction, and left you hanging there, unfulfilled.

Once, when I was about five years old, and my mother knelt down to dry me off after a bath, I hung my arms around her neck. I pretended to do it so that every inch of me was accessible to the toweling off, but it was really because that was the closest thing I could get to a hug from her. I had to steal it. And like a kid on a shopping spree in Toys R Us, I tried to get it all at one time: I stole a kiss, too.

I expected her to squeeze me in for a tighter hug, and lavishly return my affection with little kisses all over my face and neck. After all, that's what the *Brady Bunch* mom did on TV.

Instead, my mother looked at me in horror, like I had slapped her face instead of pecked her lips. She wiped the kiss off with the back of her hand, and said, "Stop that foolishness, now. I don't have time for that. I got four other kids behind you that need bathing," and she continued to dry me off.

Undeterred and needing more, I went in for the kill. "Mama," I said with my head hanging, hands by my side now, feeling dejected and unable to look her in the eyes. "Do you love me?"

To which she wrapped the towel around me, gave me a faint smile and a quick pat on the behind and said, "Little girl, go get your pajamas on."

Years later, when I would think about that moment, I would often wonder why I hadn't said the words myself: *I love you, Mama.* What would she have done then? Would she still have left my love in the lurch, verbally unrequited?

People make choices, and those choices have consequences.

Throughout the years, I tried to understand the choices she made in regards to affection for her children and, who knows, probably her husband, my dad, as well; but the consequences of her actions were far-reaching. And that is what my letter to my mother is all about.

Dear Mommie,

I love you.

You were the one who showed me how to love. Even though you didn't express your love with words, you showed it with your deeds.

It seemed to be hard for you to verbalize the love I know you felt for me, and I never knew why. Was it because that's how you were raised? I know you were born in the middle of the Great Depression, and times were hard, especially in the Dust Bowl of rural Oklahoma. If that was the reason, I totally understand that. We sometimes raise our children the way we were raised.

Or was it because of your Native American culture? Indians as a rule aren't verbally expressive. They say what they mean with no frills added. Daddy always said you were his backwoods (and by that, I took it to mean back*wards*) country girl, and that when he came courting, you would hide behind a tree until your sisters dragged you out.

Maybe you never said *I love you* to me because of what they call fear of intimacy. That's where you don't want to get too close to people because it makes you feel vulnerable, and susceptible of hurt or rejection, which is funny because by being that way, you are, in a sense, rejecting those that *you* love. It's a conundrum. *I love you* is such a simple sentence, but it houses very complex emotions.

Yet and still, I wanted to hear it from you.

I know you were capable of saying it, so it wasn't that you couldn't. It was that you chose not to. Whether that was a conscious decision (I'm not going to tell my children I love them because that will make them weak and needy, and they need to be strong and self-reliant when they get out in the cold cruel world), or you did it subconsciously (I didn't hear it, and I'm fine; this is how you raise children), I don't know.

As a child, I felt like I was deprived of something that I figured most kids had on a daily basis, and it made me feel weak, needy and inadequate. I craved acceptance from others. It sent me through emotional changes that, for the most part, hurt while I was going through them, but in the end, it made me a better person.

As long as we live, we are supposed to grow. In order to grow, we must learn from our own mistakes as well as those around us. But we have to pay attention.

Here is what I learned from paying attention to you, my darling Mommie:

We are imperfect. That includes you, and all the rest of us mothers, daughters, presidents and popes. We sometimes get things wrong. We have human foibles, and we are not the mistakes we have made.

We also can't control what others say and do, and conversely, we can't control what others don't say and don't do. It is beyond our realm of authority to force behavior in others. That golden nugget, dear Mommie, helped me in my professional life as well as my marital life. We can, however, control our own behavior, and so I broke the cycle. I say *I love you* to my children every chance I get. I am sure my kids will grow up and correct some mistake I've made in raising them, and do something different with their children, and I'm okay with that.

Remember that song your favorite singer Judy Garland used to croon, "You Made Me Love You"? Well, you made me love you *and* myself. To this day, I care little about whether other people like me or not, because I love me. I finally accepted myself, and realized that you not saying those three little words was not because of anything I did or did not do. You did the best you could with what you had.

Because of all those things, I finally accepted you, too, for who you are, a mother who lived her love out loud, but kept the words to herself.

So imagine my surprise when you began that slow crawl toward end-stage kidney failure, and you called each of your children into your hospital room one at a time. None of us knew what you said to the other, but I know what you told me: "I love you, Leenie."

When I heard those three wonderful words, I felt like you had been saying them my whole life, and in many ways you had. And so I simply replied, "I love you, too, Mommie."

Some people might think that was too little, too late, but I think it was just enough, at just the right time.

I Will Miss You Always.

Arlene

After thirty years as a court reporter in Los Angeles Superior Court, Arlene L. Walker is now embarking on her dream career of being a novelist. She is a graduate of the UCLA Writer's Program, and a 2010 PEN USA Emerging Voices finalist. Her short stories have received Honorable Mentions in 78th *Writer's Digest Writing Competition of 2009, and the 2012 Palm Springs Writer's Guild Short Story Contest. She currently has her nose to the grindstone working on her debut novel,* Feather Falls.

Mother Envy
Pamela Samuels Young

"You don't look nothin' like your mama."

As an introverted, awkward pre-teen, I heard those words quite often from both family and friends. Each time, they stung deeply. I would promptly hang my young head and wonder why God hadn't made me in the spitting image of my beautiful mother.

A picture of petiteness, Pearl (even her name conjures up a sense of something delicate) is just a smidgen over five feet. In contrast, by the time I'd reached middle school, one cousin had nicknamed me the Jolly Green Giant. And standing next to my mother, that's exactly how I felt. Her dainty size-six frame and size-five feet made playing dress-up in her closet next to impossible. I've never been able to get a single toe of my size eight-and-a-halves into one of her fancy pumps. I don't think my waist was twenty-one inches even in second grade.

My mother has shiny, naturally curly hair that's never required a straightening comb or a relaxer. I, however, did not have *good* hair. I spent many a Saturday morning hunched in a kitchen chair, holding my ears flat to my face as my mother attacked my naps with a sizzling hot, giant-sized pressing comb.

Pearl is also a striking woman. Her skin is a shade or so lighter than maple syrup, but just as smooth in texture. I've never seen her bother with mascara or eyeliner. For Pearl, foundation is an option, not a necessity. The natural look, however, doesn't work for me. I rarely leave the house without a quick workout with the arsenal of cosmetics in my makeup bag. My mother, on the other hand, glides some lipstick across her pert lips and is on her way. I can't recall ever seeing a pimple on her face and she rarely complains about her skin. Why would she? It's flawless. Even today, my face still bears the scars of the severe acne that was partly responsible for my adolescent shyness.

As the years passed, so did my bashfulness. Time and age have allowed me to become more confident in my own skin. Fortunately for me, I'm no longer embarrassed about my height. It wasn't until I got to college that I came to realize that five-six is more average than tall, and my feet aren't really all *that* big. They just seemed that way next to Pearl's tiny feet. And my hair? I now truly adore my naturally kinky coils.

Though I can honestly say I'm happy with the woman I am today, I still envy my remarkable mother. Now, though, a whole different set of reasons are the source of that envy.

Dear Mama,

I envy you. Not your lovely skin or your little feet. Not your curly hair or your petite frame. These days, I envy those ways of yours that I didn't pay much attention to as a child. I'm talking about those personal qualities that you display with the grace of a queen. Qualities that have allowed you to reach the age of eighty-two with a smile on your face and a song of praise in your heart each and every day.

For one, I envy your strength.

I must admit that in my youth, I didn't necessarily think of you as a strong woman. After all, you're a little bitty lady. But with the hindsight of my own life experiences, I now see the vastness of your inner and outer strength.

I've had a pretty charmed life, thanks to you and Daddy. Your hard work made it possible for me to accomplish my dreams of becoming a lawyer, and later, a novelist. I've often wondered what big dreams you had for yourself back in 1950 when you left Atlanta and boarded Amtrak headed for California. You were only eighteen years old when you arrived in Watts. While your life was ultimately a good one, I suspect that you did not expect to spend twenty-five years as a mail carrier, enduring swollen feet, intense back pain and occasional dog bites. But you did what you had to do for your family. You did what you had to do for me. That took strength.

I've watched you *handle* my daddy, the man you've been married to for sixty-plus years. And no matter how right or how wrong he may be, you never lose your cool.

"You know how your daddy is," you say, with a wave of your hand. "I don't pay him any mind."

Always the picture of calm in the face of calamity, I can count on one hand the number of times I've heard you raise your voice. As I wrestle with my own marital ups and downs, I think about how you'd handle the situation and struggle to find the mental strength to zip my lips, as you would do, when that might diffuse the situation.

"Don't sweat the small stuff," I've heard you say many times.

If there's ever any family strife, you're always the first to remind us: "Don't worry about it. God will fix it."

I've also marveled at the way you've handled your own personal challenges. Like the heartbreak of a miscarriage and not being able to finish that college degree you started because of your family obligations. I've watched you bury your parents and raise multiple foster children you had to love, then let go. That took strength.

I also envy your giving spirit.

You never hesitate to lend a helping hand to anyone in need: friend, family or stranger.

During your many years as a mail carrier, you did a lot more than deliver the mail. You brought sunshine to the families in the Athens Park community—many of them elderly—who were lucky enough to have you as their mail lady. You cared for them and watched over them like they were family.

Despite the ribbing from your co-workers who said you were being taken for a ride, you loaned two thousand dollars to a woman on your route who was about to lose her home.

"I felt her spirit," you told me.

Though she never got around to paying it all back, you didn't fret.

"God will bless me in other ways," you said.

Worried about another homeowner who hadn't been around to greet you for a few days, you took it upon yourself to check on her safety. You entered her back door and found her stretched out on the floor in need of help.

I've watched you constantly give of yourself to your family, expecting nothing in return. At the age of twenty-two, I didn't fully understand the significance of your writing a huge check to pay one hundred percent of my tuition for graduate school at Northwestern University. While other students with families who had far more than we did were forced to get student loans, I finished my education debt free. I didn't know that you had wiped out a significant chunk of your retirement savings. But you never had a second thought about doing so.

Finally, most of all I envy your unyielding faith in God. While I'm now on my third church home, you have been a diehard member of Community Baptist Church in Compton, California, for over forty-five years. *That* is commitment. Despite all the ups and downs that church folks can sometimes send you through, you never considered leaving *your* church. I always know where I can find you on Sunday mornings: far left side, corner seat, third pew from the pulpit.

I thank you for showing me by example the power of prayer. Although I sometimes loathed being dragged off to Sunday school, regular church service and *then* the evening program, I now see that those experiences were the building blocks of my faith. Without them, I don't know where I'd be.

It's been difficult for me to think about the fact that one day you won't be here for me. That's why I kept putting you off every time you brought up the subject of talking about your *arrangements*. Unlike me, you have no fear of death.

Conjuring up some of the strength I've seen you exhibit, I finally found the courage to have that conversation. I listened—quite uncomfortably—surprised at all the effort that you'd given to your earthly goodbye. You calmly pointed out where I could find the important papers, the precise location of your cemetery plot, and who I should call at the church. Rest assured that I will follow each and every one of your very specific, handwritten instructions. And yes, Mama, I'll definitely make sure somebody sings "May the Work I've Done Speak for Me."

Though I've always known you were a woman of God, I don't think I truly understood the depth of your faith until we had that conversation. Yes, you will be sad to leave us, but you will be overjoyed to meet Jesus.

It still makes me smile when I recall your final directive on this topic: "I don't want a funeral service," you told me. "I want a homegoing celebration."

I promise, Mama, I'll do all I can to make sure you have the biggest, most spirit-filled homegoing that Community Baptist Church has ever seen. And while I know I will cry buckets of tears, I will find comfort in the knowledge that I was raised by a mother whose generous spirit would give Mother Teresa a run for her money, whose strength could push aside any mountain in her path, and whose faith rivals Job's.

While I can't exactly say God has allowed you to pass on those traits to me—at least not as abundantly as he bestowed them upon you—He did finally answer the prayers of that gawky little girl who longed to look like her mother.

These days, I'm tickled pink every time I get a chance to visit your home away from home, Community Baptist Church, the place where I was baptized over four decades ago. Undoubtedly, someone will greet me with a welcoming smile, pull me into a bear hug and say: "You look just like your mama!"

Thank you, Pearl, for being my mother.

Love you,

Pamela

Pamela Samuels Young is a practicing attorney and bestselling author of multiple legal thrillers, including Anybody's Daughter, Murder on the Down Low, *and* Every Reasonable Doubt. *The Compton, California, native is a former journalist, and a graduate of USC, Northwestern University and UC Berkeley's School of Law.*

You'll Never Be Doris Day

Jelen Hunter

Dear Mom,

Even addressing this letter is difficult for me. I truly don't know what to call you. I sometimes feel like calling you by your first name, but that seems disrespectful (more in the sense of society's "respect your elders" protocol, and not because you are deserving of any reverence). When I was growing up, my friends half-jokingly called you "Mommy Dearest," but that still does not fit you. You are no Joan Crawford. One of your other children referred to you as "Satan." But that implies pure malevolence, when at least some of your behavior is the result of bad brain chemistry. No, none of these titles really sums you up, and most seem to give you more respect and relevance than you deserve. But the word "Mom" comes pre-loaded with images of maternal affection and unconditional love. Or even as a protector of the innocent. But you never seemed to embody any of those common motherly traits. Although you physically gave birth to me, you were never truly my "mother."

Blinded by mania and narcissism, I wonder if you ever truly recognized that you were someone's mom; or if, as your child, I was a mere annoyance to you. I was just someone who kept the constant revolving-door of social workers coming to the house, for whom you would put on a good show, acting above reproach for the hour they observed us. I sometimes believed all of the things you said to those visitors—that you would be a better mom, or that you would not scream or hit me. But once suspicion of your behavior had driven off with each LCSW, everything returned to the status quo.

When I was really little, you locked me in my room for hours and sometimes days, as you pondered what to do with me. I was entirely too curious and intelligent to be out amongst you and the constant barrage of male visitors. But when I was ten years old, the tides changed. I had by then become cognizant and fairly independent. It was then that you asked me to be your best friend. You were convinced that we could tell people that you were my older sister. And although I rebuffed this request as that of a desperate woman, it did signify a change in our relationship. I felt sorry for you. Suddenly I became the caregiver. I became your "mother." I was shoe-horned by your constant guilt-trips, codependence, sadness and distress into acting as the responsible adult in our relationship. Essentially my childhood was stripped from me. Someone had to be the responsible party, and as you were having none of it, I stepped up—and I never stopped.

As I have grown older, and seen how most mothers act toward their children, I have grown bitter and disgusted. Through my gravest challenges, my greatest achievements, even near-death experiences—I had no one to turn to for support. I was alone to fend for myself. Your life was simply too important for us to take a moment to reflect on what I was facing. No, through heartbreak, failure, miscarriages, surgeries—as well as my graduations, wedding, and promotions—I was completely on my own. I had no compass; there was no great sage to answer all of the questions I had. I had no personal cheerleader. All I had was me.

But if I'd had a mother that was functional and stable? I would ask her this: When do I know it is time to give up on my dreams? And when do I stop feeling like an awkward teenager masquerading as an adult, and actually start to be comfortable in my nearly four-decade-old skin? And will I ever be successful? Or have I peaked—with no option but to accept that I have realized my highest point in society?

I know other mothers might raise concern over these questions. Likely unable to answer them, other moms might take a positive approach and say that one should never stop reaching for the stars, or that one's dreams could be realized anytime during the journey of life. You? You would smoke your cigarettes, skillfully turning the conversation to you and your problems, ignoring my needs.

I reflect on where you came from. The daughter of an immigrant municipal transportation employee and a downtown shop girl, you grew up poor, especially in comparison to the celebrities that lived just one major street north of you. At one point you were cast as a child in a big Hollywood movie—and big dreams and dollar signs appeared in everyone's eyes. But nothing ever came of it. No, you eventually married while still a teenager, and although you had visions of grandeur ahead of you (including traveling abroad and performing some exotic job requiring multiple languages), you gave up on everything. I know it was about this time that you had your first psychotic break. Maybe that is why you decided to never work and to stay sealed-up within the confines of a house your parents financed for you (and for your blue-collar, veteran husband). I wonder if this is when you knew you would never be rich or successful. Maybe the cosmos gave you a sign that you would never amount to anything and that it was better not to try.

As a child, I remember being poor. I remember dad going to Union meetings while we got very little money for food—as he walked the picket line for better benefits. Even then I understood how important it was for him to sacrifice for the greater good. We drank our water with milk powder, ate our Spam, and gladly took the opportunity to eat reconstituted Campbell's Soup with its "flavor crystals" (chunks of undissolved MSG). I wonder if dad ever saw the writing on the wall, and knew that he had to carry on at that point. That he had to keep on forcing himself to be strong—that he could see the finish line up ahead and all he needed was to push on a little bit further.

I'll never know what motivated my dad during those very lean years, but I do know that somewhere, later in life, he decided he was done. He refused promotions that were offered to him over and over again, and he eventually let the company he served for forty years force him into early retirement. Somewhere along the way he knew that he was never meant to be a leader or a middle-class worker. No, his place was in the dungarees, servicing equipment while someone else managed the team.

But I have no one to ask these questions. At my bachelorette party I sang Doris Day's "Que Será Será," in what was likely a pathetic and overtly expressive outpouring of emotion for such a formulaic Hollywood movie tune. I have heard it was epic. I only know it was sincere. Will I be pretty? Will I be famous? Will I be rich? These are questions I always asked myself, as I had no mother to ask. And at the time I still had visions of being all these things. But now I wonder if it isn't time to accept my fate.

Perhaps I excelled further than you ever dreamed possible, Mom. I *am* the first person in our family to graduate college. I *am* the first person in our family to work a white-collar job. Both of these things were made possible by the bolstering of one very supportive social worker during my teenage years—she packed love and support into the void you never attempted to fill. She encouraged me; she listened to my questions; she let me sound-off when needed.

She was probably the closest thing to a parent I ever had. I wish I could ask her when she knew to stop trying to be a French translator and to get her license for social work instead. When did she know her dreams would never be realized? When did she know to stop reaching for the stars?

I look around at my friends. We are at that age where grandparents have long passed and mortality is barreling down on our parents. Everyone else around me seems to still dream of a better life. Perhaps their parents kept the truth from them, like pretending there is a Tooth Fairy or Easter Bunny to prevent tears and disillusionment. There seems to be a need amongst my peers to believe that things can magically get better. That if you work hard enough, you, too, can lift yourself from poverty and be the next Charlie Chaplin or J.K. Rowling. Sadly, I am cynical. I see this as a pipe dream, springing leaks left and right. The people who have made it are the rare exception. If everyone could lift themselves from the caste they were born into, we would have no socioeconomic classes. No, at some point everyone must know when they have reached the highest level they can. That moment when, eventually, the writing on the wall says: This is the best you will ever be.

Mom, I wish you had taught me the skill to be able to convince myself of the lie that is hope; that dreams never die, and that I can still be a seismologist, or professor, or journalist if I just apply myself. I wish that you had told me that opportunity really does exist for everyone, regardless of how much money you have, or who you know. That like George Bailey in *It's a Wonderful Life*— I can lasso the moon and make it tangible. But even more so, I wish I'd had a mom. A mother. Even Mommy Dearest. Someone who would tell me a white lie so I would never give up; someone who would encourage me to get back up after falling down; someone who could be positive for me, no matter how dire the situation I found myself in. Because sometimes it would be nice to be told, "You can be *whatever* you want to be. You can be *whoever* you want to be. Yes, you *will* be famous. Yes, you *will* be rich. Yes, there *will* be rainbows, day after day. Great things lie ahead."

   Sincerely,

   Jelen

Jelen Hunter graduated from the University of California, Santa Cruz with a degree in Literature and moonlights as a writer and editor. She lives in the Bay Area with her husband.

Dear Mable

Lori Bryant-Woolridge

My mother, Mable Maria Bryant, God bless her loving heart, is still very much alive and willfully kicking. She is healthy and beautiful, looks a decade younger than her eighty-five years, and while her body is aging, it is, gratefully, without disease. Mom has always been a quietly competitive soul, and even now, she is fighting the impending ravishes of aging by keeping her mind and body as active as they will allow. A couple of Christmases ago, she asked for a Kindle and book on comparative religions. She's an avid reader, belongs to the neighborhood book club, is computer literate and still does the annual taxes for her household. Athletically inclined, her tennis playing ended four years ago after an attempted grand slam went awry, resulting in a wrist-shattering, career-ending injury. Tennis racket tucked away, my mom still walks and regularly attends water aerobics classes. Trust me when I tell you that when it comes to physical activity, the old girl puts me to shame!

I suppose all of this physical stamina is the continuation of that needed to raise five children. Despite working full-time most of our childhood, Mom found the time to be somebody's Cub Scout leader, PTA president, and team or class mom. She was at every ballet and piano recital, football, softball and basketball game. People laugh when I tell them that we were the original Huxtables, but we were—a large, busy family who played, fought and loved together every day before sitting down to a home-cooked dinner every night. My mom was the glue that held us together and allowed us to blossom—and blossom we did. She and my dad produced a Brigadier General, a sought-after prosthetics designer, an Emmy-award-winning writer, and a successful engineer and lawyer. They did good.

In the twenty-three years I've been raising my own children, I've often wondered, how did she do it? How did she manage to work full-time, run a household, all the while be an outstanding wife and mother? The only answer that really makes sense is my mother lived a lifetime of sacrifice. She willingly forfeited her own needs, desires, and dreams for the good of her family. For this, I am forever grateful because her sacrifices provided me a storybook childhood, set me up for a long-term marriage, and gave me the tools to raise my own children, who as I type this, appear to be well on the road to becoming, successful, productive individuals. Yes, we truly prospered, but at what cost to her?

Truth be told, I am a different kind of mother in several ways. Yes, I made sacrifices for my children, but not at the magnitude of my mother's. And in the last few years, as I have gone from full-time mother to empty nester, I find my relationship with my children shifting from mother/child to mother/friend, particularly with my daughter. This shift has also cast a spotlight on my own mother/daughter relationship. After living fifty-four years with one of the kindest, most loving moms in the world, I have discovered that I barely know the woman who is my mother. The following letter is to the woman behind the apron, the chauffeur's and nurses' caps.

Dear Mable,

As our Christmas visit ends this year, and you and Daddy head back to Arizona, I want you to know that having you is all the gift

I will ever need. You have been an amazing mother. I couldn't have asked for better, nor would I change a thing.

It is so clear to me how I became the mother I am today. Watching you and directly experiencing your mothering style, I learned several important lessons about maternal love and devotion. I learned to love my children firmly but fairly, and to support and nurture them as individuals. I tried to teach them many of the same values you taught me, and like you, gave them room to test themselves and their own judgment, making sure to always be there if they needed me. As best I can tell, the lessons you passed down to me like a treasured family recipe, have produced two fine, productive young adults. So thank you from the bottom of my heart for leading by example.

I have noticed that as Eva ages and we morph into BFFs (with healthy parental boundaries), our conversations have taken on a more woman-to-woman tone. We talk about everything—love, sex, relationships. These talks have allowed me to reveal myself to my daughter as a person not must a mom. I give Eva my opinions and advice when asked (okay, sometimes unsolicited), and try to share with her lessons I've learned through my own experience. I see my influence in some of her decisions and actions. Reflecting back on these talks, I realized that because of the very private person you are, we never really had many of these conversations throughout the years. Some of this may be my fault. I've always seen you as way more conservative, religious and rigid than myself. Perhaps I thought you wouldn't understand my points of view. More than likely, though, I didn't want to disappoint you by my actions. Whatever the reasons, the end result was that we've spent most of our lives loving and respecting each other madly as mother and daughter, while circling each other as familiar strangers.

You know that old saying that if you want to know what a girl is going to look like when she gets old, look at her mother? I've always had that category nailed. From as far back as I can remember, people have told me that I look just like you. I recall in my teen years the great annoyance I felt whenever I heard that comment. I was trying so hard to find my own sense of self that I rejected such observations out of hand. I apologize if you ever felt slighted or hurt. And please know how proud I am now to bear your designer "genes." There are times when I look in the mirror and see your face looking back at me. At first it was kind of scary, now it's quite comforting. I can only hope that I look as good as you do in thirty years.

As I sat down to write this letter and reflected on our relationship, the thought occurred to me that while we do bear a striking physical resemblance and have similar mothering styles, I am a far different woman than you. Or at least I've spent most of my adult life thinking so.

You go to church every Sunday, follow the rules of your Catholic religion and never take the Lord's name in vain. I love God, but never go to church, swear like a sailor and think FUCK is one of the best words in the English language. You skip the "dirty" parts in the books you love to read, while I not only enjoy reading them, but write and publish erotic novels. Prior to getting married, you were a virgin, and thought I'd be the same. Clearly, that didn't pan out and we'll just leave it at that. You are sweetly naïve when it comes to sex, and I take delight in reading, studying and experiencing it for my own pleasure but also to coach other women how to revel in their desires. "Modesty" is your middle name. I've adopted "Sexy" as mine. You spend your career as a nurse, nurturing others and teaching others how to take care of themselves. I've spent the last thirteen years as a writer and sensuality coach, teaching women how to find their feminine confidence and unique brand of sexy. Certainly we're at opposite ends of the career spectrum.

A big turning point for me was the cruise we took together in 2006 to celebrate Eva's thirteenth birthday. It was there, sailing the beautiful Caribbean Sea, that with much shock and awe, I began to see you as a woman instead of simply my mother. I came to some startling revelations on that trip—revelations that made me understand that we have much more in common as women than I ever believed.

As this was our first "just the girls" trip together, I didn't know what to expect. I was prepared to "babysit" both you and Eva, but actually neither one of you needed keeping up with. Each morning you were up bright and early to walk the deck, and by the time you met us for breakfast, you had a list of activities planned for the day—dance lessons, lectures, shows. You were like an uncaged bird—flitting around when and where you chose, free at last to bear witness to the world around you on your own terms. Without knowing it, you had passed the test of any girlfriend I travel with—the ability to entertain yourself. I learned that you, like me, were comfortable venturing out alone to explore and enjoy the world around you. You'd meet us again at lunch to show us the banana dance you'd learned or share stories about fellow cruisers you'd met during the day. I realized on that trip that we are both very confident, independent women. The difference has been that I have always been very forthright about claiming my slice of independence within my marriage. But because of the times you were raised and married in, you weren't able to do so, and were forced to shut down that very vibrant side of you for the sake of husband and family. Oh, but that light of independence shines as bright in you as it does in Lady Liberty.

And who knew that you had such a breadth of intellectual and cultural curiosity? As a writer, I have always been interested in and fascinated by people, places and things at home and abroad. This curiosity fuels my writing and enriches my life. Could it be that I inherited my natural inquisitiveness from you? It appeared that way on the cruise, not only by the pertinent questions you asked during conversations with fellow passengers and tour guides, but by the amount of research you did on the places we were visiting before you even left home. And as Eva and I lazed around the pool on our sea days, you were busy enjoying everything from classes on creating towel animals to lectures on island history. I listened as you voiced your opinion on religion and politics and other matters with a wit and fire I'd rarely seen around our dinner table. It became obvious to me on that trip that like me, you cannot get enough of the world around you. Also, just as beautifully glaring was that you really do have opinions, and I love and admire that about you.

And until that trip, I had no idea what a natural flirt you are! Is it that I'd never noticed before or was this simply the first time we'd spent this much time together without Daddy? I've always prided myself on being a great flirt. So good that other women pay me to teach them how to charm and disarm. And the foundations of my lessons have always been that flirting is never about wanting anything from anybody. It's about making other people feel good about who they are in your presence. Omigod, Mable! You are a master! You were never at a loss for a dance partner or a fellow conversationalist. I watched as the cabin stewards, waiters and the like fell victim to your charms, and you didn't even realize what you were doing! It was an awesome display of feminine wit and wiles. Who knew?

I also learned on a stroll through an outdoor market on one of the islands that you have a secret sexuality about you that I had never fathomed. We passed a table selling beautiful lace lingerie and I teased you about picking up a few pieces to surprise Daddy. You shook your head and with a wistful look in your eyes, told me about the time, many decades ago, that you'd slipped into something much more sexy and daring than your usual flannel nighties, and had gotten a very negative reaction from your husband. To ease the moment, I teased you about there being a secret freak underneath all of those good girl layers. The subtle but sly smile you gave me said it all. In a different place and time, perhaps with a different man, and you might have been seriously getting your freak on! So, maybe you haven't been skipping all the naughty pages in those books you've been reading!

That cruise taught me so much about myself and you, a beautiful and talented woman. I watched you find joy in every place you stood on that trip. Whether you were watching a bunch of silly men dressed up as women for a passenger show or witnessing the magnificent sunset, you *lived* every moment of those ten days at sea. I also realized that we both loved the same thing about cruising, the chance to get back to our true selves without the sometimes heavy tags of mother and wife hanging around our necks. For those ten days we were two friends afloat, enjoying the true essence of who we are as women.

Since that trip, and in the six years that followed, it has become clear to me that not only do I look like you, I am you in so many more ways than I ever imagined. On our cruise last year to the Mediterranean to celebrate Eva's eighteenth birthday, our friendship was deepened by the common bond of passing the torch of girl to woman from mother to daughter. We enjoyed that cruise as three generations of sexy, vibrant, fabulous women. And as I witnessed my own daughter stepping into my stilettos as the pretty, young thing in the family, I could look to you and take comfort in the fact that my journey was a long way from being over, and the best was yet to come.

While working as a sensuality coach and advising women how to find and feel comfortable and confident in their own brand of sexy, people often ask me how I become the woman I am. I used to think that I was simply a product of nature. It turns out that I am who I am due to your nurturing. This was a concept that didn't truly make sense to me until recently. While I was growing up, you dutifully gave me the facts about love, dating and sex, but we never discussed the emotional joys and sorrows of love or the pleasure principles of great sex. It was understood that such discussions were taboo. I never saw you in sexy lingerie or stilettos or any garb that indicated that you were a sexual being.

But now I know that you taught me, through action not words, how to become the woman that you were not allowed to be. You did not fill my head up with over-reaching rules and boundaries, but rather solid values and self-confidence. Growing up, you gave me all of the tools necessary to paint the kind of life I wanted to live, while at the same time letting me remain a fairly blank canvas. You understood your limits and allowed me to explore my own by loving me enough to share me with other women whose outlooks and ideas varied widely from yours. I was free to find myself, buoyed by the knowledge that your love was unconditional. You let me fall, while never letting me believe I'd failed, and were always there to pick me up. What a clever mother and amazing woman you are!

Thank you, Mable, for being my friend, mentor and mother. I

love you with all of my heart and now proudly shout to the world that I am just like my mother!

Love,

Lori

Lori Bryant-Woolridge is an author, sensuality coach, and founder of Stiletto U, a virtual university that advocates healthy, sensual lifestyles. She is the author of The Power of Wow: A Guide to Unleashing the Confident Sexy You, *and has authored three* Essence *best-selling novels, including* Weapons of Mass Seduction. *She is the editor of the erotic anthology,* Can't Help the Way That I Feel.

A Saint in Everyday Clothes
Joanne C. Hillhouse

Tanty died when I was a little girl. From her I inherited the name she had given me, Joanne; the silver bracelets I still wear; and a black and white notebook about a quarter filled with her elegant script.

When I got that book I thought the words were hers, and I filled the rest of its pages with my words as though writing in response to what I found there. On the pages of that weathered black and white book, there were the ramblings of a child and the makings of a plantation era fiction, inspired no doubt by what she'd written down—in the way that one writes down favorite Bible verses. I learned that they were not in fact written, as I thought then, by her.

That book is a thin thread of connection to the woman who filled the emotional spaces in our lives with steadiness and kindness and strength and comfort, and it is an early indication of what I would become, a writer. She had something to do with that.

It's probably fitting then that she haunts my writing.

In my first book, *The Boy from Willow Bend*, the Tanty character is completely modeled on her. It's rare in my fiction for someone to be on the page exactly as they are in life. Sure, I might unconsciously/subconsciously grab bits and pieces of things; someone's smile, or the way they move, or their speech patterns. In the case of my most recent book, *Oh Gad!*, my memory of Mama, my paternal grandmother's towering stature and implacability became a partial model for Mama Vi. Apart from the fact that they both worked at coal pot making, the details of the character's life, are all invented, however. My books are fiction for a reason. They may, as I said in a poem once, "steal" from life, but they are not a literal reflection of my life or the lives of anyone I know; except in the case of Tanty in *The Boy from Willow Bend*. Even then, literal is relative because we're talking about a child's memory of a person not as opposed to precisely who that person was. In life and on the page, who that person was to the child I was then and to the titular Boy Tanty was an anchor in a sometimes confusing and fast-moving world. In *the book* and in life, Tanty was a generous and beautiful spirit married to a man that was bursts of thunder in counterpoint to her steady calming breeze. Without bitterness at her own barren womb, she raised the children her husband had with other women, children like my mother, and loved them as if they were her own. She was firm without ever being loud, and faithful to the painful end. The Tanty character left a void when she died. All of that was my Tanty right up to, and including the scene, where they took her body away.

"...sat on the front step and people just stepped around him. He cried. Heavy, silent tears, grown up tears. A woman he didn't know pulled him up and to her, hugging him close. And he cried into the soft comfort of her belly."

That moment is taken completely from my memory of Tanty's dying and everything described is my lasting impressions from that day, that moment.

Throughout, the book mimes my fragmented images and imprecise recollections of Tanty, of Camacho's Avenue (reinvented as Dead End Alley-cum-Willow Bend), my first memory of home, and of family lore (not any one person's particular story, just puzzle pieces that came together in this fiction). I say fragmented and imprecise because as a child, not enough of the details of Tanty's life would have been known to me beyond what was observed and said in passing; but enough lives that I was able to flesh her together on the page.

When she read the book, my one-year-older sister, not known for being effusive with her compliments, sent me this via email: "I do believe you have a masterpiece. I think the book has taken me back in time a lot. Tanty's dying all over again, however, made me cry. She was such a peaceful soul. You are truly a talented being. Djeri wanted to know if you wrote the book all by yourself and why?" My then infant niece's puzzlement over why I would have written a book and my sister's unfamiliar praise made this one of my favorite responses to anything I've written. I *sheroe* worshipped my sister as a kid. But then there's Tanty. I loved that she saw what I'd written for what it was; that Tanty lived still with all of us, on the page and, in our memories.

There's an old African proverb, "no one truly dies until no one remembers you." If this is true, almost thirty years on from her death, at this writing, Tanty is still very much alive.

Here are a few examples just from the past few weeks:

I was asked about presenting at a literary conference at which one of the sub themes is memory, and the abstract I submitted was entitled "Mi Tanty Haunting Me." I thought in grabbing hold of that theme, not just of *The Boy from Willow Bend* but of so many other areas of my writing where she pops up; whether her quiet determination, the force of her love, her resourcefulness, or the way, as I once wrote in a poem:

"*Saturday*
was Market Day
with Tanty
head wrapped tight
like some Dominica
country woman
long plantation style
dresses
stresses
stooping
her shoulders
smiling away
the creases
that old people
wear to mark
the years
'*til she seemed*
almost like a girl
again.
And she was never without her halo."

Almost as soon as I suggested "Mi Tanty Haunting Me" as my theme for the conference, I began to worry about it, as I worried about writing about her for this chapter. Because I didn't know if I could do this, i.e. consciously choose to write about her, *memoir-ish-like. The Boy from Willow Bend* aside, when she inserts herself into my fiction, it doesn't happen in a conscious way, it happens instinctively because she is always with me like an angel-editor. I didn't want to exploit that relationship or expose her to any kind of unkind scrutiny. I feel protective of her as she was protective of us, all of us, including my mother, in our childhood.

My mother, she's the other reason Tanty's been on my mind these past weeks. I don't know if she's conscious of it, but she references Tanty a lot. Now, I think my mother is another reason I am a writer. Some of the first books I read were pilfered from her stash. Plus, she has a way with colorful phrases that has me grabbing for my pen like when in a fit of temper at the competence of this or that person, she'll scoff:

"Dem can't run nothin'
All dem can run ah fowl."

That's not something I would have come up with, but I might use it. There is the fact that so many of my characters have mommy issues and I'll just leave that there. There is the fact that all of her important lessons came in the form of parables. Like, growing up, she wouldn't just tell us to be satisfied with what she gave us and not beg or eat from others; she'd tell us the story of some bright student who took a piece of sugar cake from somebody and has been a vegetable ever since…or something. Her stories are the tall tales and superstitions of her own childhood, passed on to her children, and now the Gospels of Tanty are added to the litany. So that when I was down recently about my progress through life, she said:

"Tanty does say say…'the rich will get poorer and the poor will come rich…' It will happen but we don't have time!"

And by time, there, she means patience, faithfulness, which Tanty had in spades, right up to her painful end.

My brother and I spoke about her these past weeks, about that faithfulness. If I feel any bitterness about Tanty's life, it has to do with how she suffered at the end. There's a little girl inside of me still stomping her foot, declaring, it's not fair; it's not fair that someone who gave so much to everyone, who sacrificed for everyone and had so little in return in her life, should be ripped apart by cancerous pain in the weeks, days, and hours of her death. It's not fair. I said this to my brother recently. That while the little Catholic girl I was then was unlikely to question God to his face, a part of me grumbled in the way that children do behind their parents' back about the unfairness of it, a part of me thought that she deserved a peaceful passing, in her sleep maybe, and wondered why God couldn't have given her that. And he, my brother, said he never looked at it like that; he preferred to think of it as God's final test, God's confidence in her strength, in her ability to endure the worst that life could throw at her. It was a testament to her strength, he said.

My mother, one of the children she raised, who was not her own, cared for her at the end, and often my sister and I were with her so we heard every pained moan, and it hurt. But even then Tanty remained faithful. So maybe my brother is right. It's a comforting way to think of it anyway.

After that conversation with my brother, I wrote something on Facebook; no, not because we seem to live our lives on Facebook these days but because I wanted to let her know how present she still was in my life. I wanted to honor her in some public way. So I wrote:

"The problem with reminiscing about those who are gone as my brother and I did yesterday is you realize how much you miss them. Tanty, in your living you taught us kindness and endurance, and your dying still causes fresh pain all these years later. But tonight you're reminding me that nothing I go through is as great as what you endured; tonight, I feel you challenging me not to break no matter what life throws at me. Missing you and keeping you alive the only way I can and in my heart always. In my dreams you wear a halo."

I commented, as people responded to that thread, that when I was little I thought Tanty was her name and would only later discover that she was Clarice. She was Tanty, the creolized version of auntie, in the way that all Caribbean matriarchs who are not your mother are Tanty, out of respect. With the ways she filled up our lives and the way she fills our memories still, Tanty lives in the place where mothers live, though she was my mother's stepmother and my step-grandmother, because she mothered us all into the beings we are now, with love and steadiness and always a calmness of spirit.

So if she haunts my fiction, if she haunts our lives still, then it's a good haunting. Because you see, in my family, we don't agree on much, but we agree on this—Tanty is a saint. And in our world, saints sometimes wear everyday dresses, and tie their heads at night and stuff it with soursop leaves. And we love them fiercely because they taught us how to love.

Letter to Tanty

Tanty, I miss you. Your dying taught me how unfair life can be more profoundly than any memory from my childhood. I wish you could have been spared the pain you endured at the end, because I never knew anyone more generous than you. I am not half so generous, not half so calm as you somehow managed to be through the challenges of your life. How'd you do it? How'd you manage to not throw up your hands and weep at your lot?

I know I couldn't be a good wife, not in the way you were. Forgiving his indiscretions, hugging his children close, be to them the comfort and nurture that not even he was, especially not him. He was intimidating to the child I was then; talented and charismatic, but intimidating. While you, I remember sitting in your lap, and slipping my hand into yours, and hiding behind your skirt, one hand bunched into its voluminous folds. You dressed like those women way back when, those women with yards of skirt, like a grandmother, and you had a grandmother's girth, and a grandmother's aches and pains, pains that made you wrap your head with bush every night and aches that made you have us children scrape and rub your feet at night. You embraced all of us like we were your children though you never had any children of your own, a reminder that family is more than blood; it is love and sometimes it comes in the form of a wedding ring and an open heart.

And so as you raised my mother and her multiple siblings and various other children left behind by mothers who would send for them someday when they got settled overseas—generations of them—I suppose you didn't think of it as your lot, as something being done to you. You didn't have the luxury of thinking of it that way, I suppose. I don't know how lucky I am, do I? For certainly, as much *knock 'bout* as life continues to send my way, I have the luxury of saying I dream, I want, I choose. While I really don't know what you would have dreamt or wanted or chosen differently. You cooked for us—I can still smell the pungent smell of the shark frying on Sunday. You made do with very little—I can still remember running to the corner shop at nighttime clutching the pennies you always managed to scrounge up for a loaf of bread, a pack of Milo, two ounces of cheese. My brother and I joke about that now, but you made sure we didn't go to bed hungry at night, and it never occurred to us, not once, to ask if you were okay. I have no doubt then that it's from you that our mother learned how a mother must sacrifice for her children, because she sacrificed for us, and, when she could, drew other children into her care as you taught her. And, for her, the Bible is as solid an anchor as it was for you. It's weird because you're so different, you and my mother, and I fantasize that you and I would have been less combative than she and I can be, had you lived, but she carries the best of you in her, and we carry the best of you collectively in our memories. Did you know how much you influenced us?

Right now, you're trying really hard to remind me that life never puts more on you than you can take; you're trying to remind me that I can take it; that no matter what, I can get through it, that we all, of the generations still mourning you somehow, but influenced by you, can get through it. You are the example of what can be endured, with grace.

In our part of the world, a Caribbean island prone to drought, young in its independence, life was never easy. What makes us think we're so special: You don't dwell on it; you just get on with it. Right, that's what you did. That's what you would tell me maybe if you were still around to tell me anything. The women who make the most sense in my stories, that's what they do; they get on with it, and that's inspired by you—and though you're from Dominica, it's a quality I think of as being quintessentially Antiguan. That ability to focus not on what's being done to you but on doing what you need to do to get through it; you were never loud but you were always strong in that way. I am of weaker stock. The characters in my stories, the younger ones fumbling around and stumbling over their own feet, have a bit too much of me in them, I think. And so Michael needed an Uncle Wellie and Nikki needed a Tanty and a Mama Vi, and Vere needed a Tanty to remind them to keep moving through life no matter what it throws at you. As I still need you sometimes.

And yet you're here, I feel you.

In the arc of my life, there are two women at the beginning of all things. One, my mother, stands tall and holds up the sky with her shoulders as hurricane force winds blow in, and she does not bend. The other is not quite so imposing and intractable; she is, you, something warm and soft I could lean in to before it was pulled away from me and with it my childhood. Both represent a different kind of strength; and yet the older I get, the more I realize that neither of you are either of these things all the time. She is not always so strong that her shoulders don't slump; as I see age begin to set upon her, I can't avoid that truth and my own need to grow up, to grow into my own strength. As lost as I feel sometimes, wasn't she younger than me when she had me, her youngest. And you, you stood up to him when need be, when it mattered, for the children. You were forceful when you needed to be; a reminder that quiet doesn't have to mean pushover. I'm writing of you and somehow the two of you are intertwined because she is my mother, but you were our matriarch. But while she and I continue to discover each other, your strength and my love for you is more uncomplicated perhaps because it's frozen in time, in the innocence of my childhood, or maybe it would have remained as easy because of your spirit. I like to think so.

I like to think that you would have taught me to cook, as you taught me to crochet, and that in those moments, I would have shared the angst I learned to pour into my writing, and perhaps I could have been comfort to you, too, as time marched on. Perhaps we would have become friends.

The absence of you is making me angry again as I write this. Where do I put all this anger I feel? Where did you put yours? Surely you must have felt brittle and angry, enraged, sometimes; how did you manage to lock it away and exude nothing but love? I never remember you raising your voice or your hand, in a world where this was the common way to engage with children. Am I romanticizing you? Because how could softness and strength exist so easily side by side. Maybe family lore is right and you were, you are, an angel.

If so, can you share some of your grace with me? Sometimes my energy, my faith, my faithfulness, everything I am waivers. Sometimes I feel the need for softness such as yours to wrap itself around me and reassure me that I'm going to be okay. I want to be weak for a minute and I know you won't judge me for it. And I need to know how to stand up and keep my feet planted as you did, to endure, as you did.

So often it feels like life is trying to get its last licks in, wondering if this is the lash that will strip me bare and leave me cowering at its feet unable to pull myself back up. And yet none of the women I looked up to, beginning with you, continuing with my mother, ever just lie there. So, I'll try to remember this, from the example you set, to be strong. I'll try to remember to be strong, as you were. I'll try to remember that even when all feels lost, giving up is not an option. I'll try to remember that. If it seems like I'm forgetting, can you just nudge me, though, with that gentle but firm touch you had?

Joanne C. Hillhouse is the author of three books, The Boy from Willow Bend, Dancing Nude in the Moonlight *and* Oh Gad! *Her work has also been published in two book-length anthologies,* For Women: In Tribute to Nina Simone *and* In the Black: New African Canadian Literature. *Hillhouse is from Antigua and Barbuda where she freelances as a writer, editor, and writing coach. She also runs the Wadadli Pen writing program.*

I've Been Meaning to Tell You

Lynda Sandoval

I was the youngest of three girls growing up in a middle-class family. A middle-class *alcoholic* family, I should say—the alcoholic in question being my father.

Fact.

I have written about this benchmark truth of my formative years, discussed it *ad nauseam* with my sisters, my mom, my cousins, my friends, and with attentive strangers in a church community room, perched on folding metal chairs and holding Styrofoam cups of bad, beige coffee.

I have risen above it and not.

I have dwelled in it and dismissed it.

I have regretted it and released it.

I have used The Big Fact as an excuse, and I have fallen into dysfunction in its various forms because of it. Or so I tell myself. I have dipped my toe into success in relationships and in my career, but I have crashed and burned and stood in my own way and made horrible choices at least twice as many times. I have allowed—yes, allowed—the nasty fact of my dad's alcoholism to both fuel my dreams and sabotage them. I have spent decades letting the fact of my dad's disease negatively impact my sense of self, of accomplishment, of worth, of ability, of stability, and of truth.

So here's another fact, and one I'm not proud of: I've focused on "the alcoholic dad thing" far more than the equally powerful, "mom who held the family together thing." The big question is, why?

I can fall back on the age-old excuse that we hear negative comments far louder than the positive ones, and this may be partially true. I may claim to be exactly like my father, a truth that is useful—not to mention convenient—to explain my many shortcomings and failures. But on the flip-side of that old, overplayed record is my mom, who has supported me, emotionally—and often financially—over the years, who has lifted me up and believed in me when I not only didn't believe in myself, but when I frankly didn't deserve it.

I've come to view Mom as the bridge truss I clung to when the river of life ran rough and high, threatening to pull me into its current and wash me away. Shivering, bone-soaked, and terrified, one doesn't focus on the strong, steady, sturdy truss. Regretfully, one tends to focus on the rage of the water. I yearn to turn my eyes away from the possibility that I've taken my mom and all her wonderfulness for granted, because it's just too horrible to ponder. But, it looms out there like a trail of crumbs begging to be followed to the stripped-bare truth at the end, and so I shall.

Before it's too late, and despite the fact that it's far too little, this is an open, honest letter to my mom, a woman who is living nobly in the perfectly imperfect life she's been given. A woman who has been able to stand anchored in optimism despite the cynical waves of the world crashing over and around her. A woman who has never grown embittered by being taken for granted by me, by my father, or by any of the many people she helped throughout the years. This is, at once, a thank you and an apology, an explanation and a cause. It's the celebration of a daughter who, yes, grew up in that middle-class, alcoholic family—bolstered and protected by the most amazing woman I have never thanked for all the ways she shaped me.

Dear Marmaduke,

Here's what irks me: It is impossible for me to write this letter to you without mentioning Dad. I don't have to recast all the ways having him as a father has molded me into the person I am today, for better or for worse, blah-blah-blah. You know all this. I'd rather focus how unworthy I feel to have someone as amazing as you for a mom, and then apologize for feeling unworthy. Yet, try as I might, I can't seem to untie Dad's thread from yours in the tapestry of my life.

So, there it is.

You and Dad. Dad and you.

The combined force that created me and Elena and Loretta in different combinations (and I can't resist the urge to point out that I believe their combos turned out much better than mine.) We've always claimed you "made up for" Dad's deficiencies as a parent, but I'm tired of that viewpoint. Dad's shortcomings shouldn't be the focus, and frankly, the older I get, the more I realize these so-called "shortcomings" were less that and more…him being him, muddling through the ups and downs of life with the same fallible humanness we all deal with.

You aren't the subplot in this epic life story of mine, please know that. I'm unspeakably sorry if I've ever made you feel that way, because here is the baseline truth: Every single thing I've ever struggled to receive from Dad, from partners, from friends and employers and readers, i.e. respect, unconditional love, enthusiastic support, faith in my abilities, you've given freely. And maybe, I took that for granted, because you're my mom. You *had* to love me, right?

I feel a desperate, scrambling urge to backtrack, rewind, rewrite. To be a better daughter, to be the person you see when you look at me, instead of the person I see and judge and beat up every time I look myself squarely in the face. But there is no backtracking. I can't even travel back in time to when I started this letter. That moment, like so many missed opportunities to be more grateful to you, is gone. I can only push forward, head down, and try to say everything I've failed to say. Right here. Right now.

Wow, big task. Already, I feel the weight of failure, something you'd no doubt admonish. I have to start at the beginning, though. Realizing there was a YOU long before there was ever a ME. It's only natural to see one's parents as capital Y, yours. But you are a woman just like me. A woman with hopes and dreams unrelated to the eventuality of me. I mean, duh. It's both obvious and not. I wish I knew more about your big, breathless dreams. About the fantasies you had for your life, what you wanted to accomplish, and if you did. What surprised you? What let you down? What are your dreams now? Maybe someday you'll tell me. I hope so. In the meantime, I will share my hopes and dreams for the rest of my life:

1. I hope I write more books, and that you love them all.

This seems like a certainty, right? I'm a writer, you're my mom. Ergo, you will dig whatever I write. Therein lies the problem. As I compose this letter, both of us are aware of the elephant in the room: that I haven't written a word of fiction for the past three years. That somewhere in between the worst break-up with the hugest relationship mistake I ever made, and the pressure of owning a house on my big, bad own and facing the reality (thankfully, untrue) that I may just spend the rest of my life alone, I froze. At first the freeze felt like a relief from the pressure to succeed, and later it got scarier, more about the pressure to not fail—something the freeze itself rendered inevitable. What if this freeze wasn't a pause, but a full stop? What if I had nothing left to say? What if

I was on the brink of huge success, but I couldn't stick it out? Couldn't cut it?

The logical part of my brain knows this isn't true, that all I have to do is start the next book and bam!—obstacle demolished, deep freeze thawed. But the frightened, inner artist part of me? Well, let's just say she doesn't know the answer to the question, will I ever write anything worthwhile again? But I'm going to try, if for nothing else than to hear that bell chime of pride ringing through your words as you tell people your daughter is an author, that your daughter has a book on the shelves at Barnes & Noble right now.

Man, all those times I chafed at you telling strangers that I was a writer, I regret. You've always been so proud of me, so enthusiastic about sharing your pride with other people, and I haven't been grateful enough. Please, fate, give me the chance to make up for that. I can only hope that I haven't damaged your faith in my abilities as I've damaged my own, what with all my negative self-talk and inaction. I have taken for granted that you'll always believe in my abilities. Now I desperately want it to still be true.

2. I hope I can repay you for all the support you've given me.

I'm humbled and embarrassed when I think of how much you've helped me financially in my adult life, and how much I squandered that gift of support for my sacred writing time. Now, as I work four jobs just to stay afloat, I can only look back at those long days I could devote to writing, all because you helped me with the details of paying my own way. This, more than anything, leaves me with the stinging slap of shame on my cheek. Please know that my wishes for success are all framed by a deep need and desire to pay it all back, the dream of being able to fund the rest of your retirement, to pay off your house, to keep you in the manner you so richly deserve. To simply pay you back.

And I hope I can repay you, also, with stories you love, all the stories you bankrolled that I failed to write because I was *burned* out. Because I was *over-stressed*. Because I heard and amplified the negative, the doubts, the disapprovals from the world and failed to turn up the volume on all the positive, the pure belief, the unwavering approval you have always given to me. I failed you—this I know. But the story hasn't ended yet, and I'm planning for a happily ever after.

3. Though I haven't always shown it, your displays of encouragement, subtle and bold, have been my lifeblood.

Dad was always extra hard on me, and I've perpetuated that lovely self-image train wreck by being extra super-duper hard on myself. You, on the other hand, supported my every whim, even my more self-destructive or misdirected or stubborn ones. And through it all, inexplicably, I've resisted embodying your vision of me; I've countered it; I've felt undeservedly pressured by your unconditional love. It's absurd. I've spent way too much time envisioning you as someone whose opinion didn't count as much, because you *had* to love me.

What a short-sighted ass I've been.

Long ago, there was a little girl who dreamed of being amazing.

And standing right next to her was a mom who already thought she was.

End of story. Right? If only life were that easy.

I want to be that person, though, Mom. I want to be the me you see. I want to be worthy of all you have ever given to me. Please know I'm trying.

4. Thank you.

I have a low-key little drawer in my office, mixed among those so-called Drawers of Greater Importance: Tax Receipts, Home Mortgage and Repair, Finances. The small drawer sits at the bottom of a stack, off to the left corner of my closet. The label on the front reads: KUDOS. For years, I've been stuffing it full with items that remind me to feel good about myself when, all too often, I let myself down in that respect.

In that drawer, you'll find fan mail from strangers, a postcard from my editor, my gold medal from the World Police and Fire Games powerlifting competition. The medal nestles next to an unevenly sliced section of a cardboard box in which my novel, *Unsettling*, was shipped from HarperCollins to bookstores and grocery stores and libraries. To see my name and book title printed on the side of a shipping crate never ceases to amaze me. But in and among all the detritus of an artistic life only partially realized are small notes from you, little jottings I've never been able to throw away. All too many of them have some variation of, "Here is your stipend for the month. Don't worry, and keep writing."

I support you.

Don't worry.

Keep writing.

Sigh.

I cherish every single note, but there is one that I love more than all the others. It is the card you sent when I sold my first book, which reads: *Congratulations. It's wonderful when good things happen to a special person like you, and I'm so glad for your success. But then, to me, you've always been a success, not just in your work, but in your relationships with others, the way you look at the world, and the way you live your life. I just wanted to remind you that I've always believed in you and let you know how proud and happy I am for you today.*

I love you. Mom.

This card sits quietly amongst a stack of congratulations cards from friends, family, editors, and my agent. It used to whisper, but now it sings, loud and clear and on pitch. You believe in me. And it's high time I start listening to that and believe in myself. It's high time I live up to that image you've always held of me. And it's high time to tell you how much having you as my mom has meant.

You didn't make up for Dad's shortcomings. Oh, no.

You loved an imperfect, but ultimately, amazing man in the best way you knew how. You lived without bitterness. You celebrated every bit of me and my sisters, even those burdens you prayed you could take from us. You created an amazing life for your three daughters, and you created three amazing daughters.

A little letter can never convey how much I love you for just being you. But for now, it's all I have.

I love you, Mom, for everything and nothing. I love you for the woman you are, and the woman you're still helping me to become.

Lynda Sandoval is an award-winning author of more than thirty books, and an editor for Bold Strokes Books. She writes women's fiction, young adult, and romance under her own name and also as Lea Santos. She has twice been named to the ALA Best Books for Reluctant Young Adult Readers' list, and was nominated for a Colorado Book Award. In her non-writing life, she works at a busy animal hospital and teaches yoga.

A Mother Sent by Providence
Pat G'Orge Walker

I was almost nine years old when my mother and I carried two
suitcases and a long shoebox filled with fried chicken and biscuits.
We were taking the Greyhound bus from Mount Vernon, New York
to Williamston, South Carolina. "You're gonna spend the summer
with your Ma Cile," my mother had told me. "I'll be back at the
end of summer and in time for you to go to class."

It was a hard lesson for a young child, but over the time, I realized
that Mama and I had different concepts of time and seasons. Seasons
changed and the years swept by and I didn't see her again but one
time until I was almost twenty years old.

I saw her that one time on the day my grandmother, Ma Cile,
buried my grandfather, Charlie. I was eleven. Ma Cile, after burying
her diabetic, multi-amputee, Alzheimer's-diseased husband, who
had given birth to seventeen children, and reared too many grandchildren to count, had finally grown weary. I was certain that my
mother would see the tiredness of her own mother and return to
New York bringing me with her.

The day after the funeral, my mother left in the dead of night.
I remember vividly how the two of us had slept on the hard wooden
floor on a pallet made of thin blankets while others slept in beds.
I'd curled up next to her just needing to hear her snore or feel her
touch. Yet she left me during that night. She'd stolen away without
kissing me, or saying so much as a "goodbye and Pat, you have fun

picking that cotton and wearing those drawers made out of flour sacks scratching your behind until blood runs; and while your belly cramps from hunger, for real; try to run as fast as you can whenever your uncle starts pawing at your young body when he can't get enough out his old wife's."

However, in between the cotton picking, physical and verbal attacks from white Southerners angered because I sat my young, black narrow behind at a lunch counter to eat the hot dog paid for from me scrubbing floors, and my hands and body too small to escape the clawing nasty perverted advances of an incestuous uncle and the constant hunger pains, there was an Angel. Her name was Ms. Bobby Madison-Mackey and she was my third-grade teacher.

As of this writing Ms. Mackey, almost eighty years old, still plays the organ at Macedonia Baptist Church in Williamston, South Carolina. She doesn't get around much without her wheelchair but still finds the time and the strength to tutor young children. And she enjoys gardening with her husband and their daughter, Bobbi.

Dear Ms. Mackey,

Here it is years later and I find you're constantly in my thoughts and prayers. As a wife, mother of three, grandmother of fourteen and great-grandmother of eight, I sometimes shudder to think of what I'd become had it not been for you.

I'm even more amazed to learn that it was my grandmother, Ma Cile, who'd encouraged you to go to college and become a teacher at the age of nineteen. I'm overwhelmed with gratitude that you took her advice and because of it—you became my third-grade teacher. You entered my life at a time when I needed someone the most. I'm at a point now where I can look back and see how God orchestrated it all. I shouldn't be surprised; there are no surprises to God or coincidences.

I want to thank you for how you took a young child battling insecurities, depression and a lack of love. A young child of nine with a very active imagination filled with farfetched details that she seamlessly wove into her life; as though knitting her own biography shaping it to provide a way to cope. You saw all of that and yet, took me into your heart.

I remember being so hungry for attention that I would follow you around the classroom. I remember making excuses not to go outside at recess with the other children. I didn't want to listen to the taunts because I wore hand-me-down everything.

I never had the twenty-five cents to eat in the lunchroom or the nickel to buy a cheese and mayonnaise sandwich. I was one of those poor wretches who sat chewing on paper pretending it was a piece of ham or a chicken leg in Ms. Sadie Wright's room. I lost count of how many days I spent there hoping one of the more prosperous children with fewer holes in their clothes would come and choose me to finish eating their leftovers. At least that way I could sit in a cold cafeteria eating real bits and pieces of food.

You never seemed to mind that I would spend time that should've been your lunch hour and tell you some of the most outrageous tales; ones that I believed were so true. I can't count the times when you sometimes stopped me and said, "C'mon, Patricia. Now you know that's not true." And I would say to you, "Oh, yes it is, Ms. Madison. I did go to the moon. When I got back, Grandpa Charlie (who had missing fingers and toes) had wrung that blue chicken's neck; and we had so much fried chicken we ate it all up. And that's why I didn't have any to bring to school today."

—And yet, there were so many days when I felt like a little princess because you'd take me aside and in front of the class, you would allow me to read to you. You'd sometimes just hold me like you knew that a touch was what I needed. The one thing you never did was to try to impede my imagination. I also remember when they took me out of your classroom saying the third grade was not a challenge for me and I should be in the fourth grade. I thank God it was a one-story school building and I was still able to visit you. You never turned me away.

I remember you with your gorgeous smile and long black hair seated in church every Sunday playing the organ. Even in that immaculate setting with praises to God resounding throughout the sanctuary, you made time to hear my latest tale. You knew long before I did that something was different about me. What you didn't know was that my imagination helped me to survive some very painful situations.

I sit here now tearing as the memories flood my mind. What an amazing woman you were and are. It's incredible to me that at that time you were but nineteen years old with so much wisdom, love and insight and how you were so unselfish with your time.

It is my desire that the entire world or any who would read my history know the miraculous part you have played in it. I especially want them to know what you told me many years later when I had published my first book, *Sister Betty! God's Calling You, Again!* You said, "Patricia, I'm not surprised you became a writer. You were the biggest liar I had in the third grade." What an amazing compliment you gave me.

Ms. Mackey, I also learned from you the power and self-gratification of giving. Whether it's time, money, advice or a simple hug or a thank-you; I know because of you the powerful impact it can have on someone or a situation. I know you had no idea what was going on at my grandmother's house and that makes me know for certain that what you did for me was all the more a part of a greater plan, God's plan.

The sad little girl that you took under your wings, nurtured by your gift of patience and caring learned to laugh. I now write novels about laughter, I tour with my one-woman comedy show, I laughed when diagnosed with cancer, I laugh when faced with all sorts of negativity. I laugh because you never allowed me to remain sad.

Thank you, Ms. Bobbie Madison-Mackey.

Pat

Pat G'Orge Walker is an Essence *and national award-winning, bestselling author, Christian comedian and playwright. She is the author of the Sister Betty gospel comedy series published by Kensington/Dafina Books and has contributed to several anthologies. She is also a former member of the legendary doo-wop group, Arlene Smith and the Chantels, as well as a veteran of the music industry having worked promotions and marketing for Epic/Columbia, Def Jam and S&D records. Pat resides in Elmont, New York.*

The Collector

Sheila J. Williams

Mothers, daughters, sisters, nieces, grandmothers, goddaughters, girlfriends, female cousins, and so it goes. The relationship dynamics between women, especially those who are in some way connected by blood or otherwise, can make you crazy. The volumes written, reality TV shows aired, oceans of tears shed and number of "I hate yous" shrieked as a result of it are legion. And at the pinnacle of the great pyramid of female relationships is the one between mothers and daughters.

"I wish that I could tell you all that I feel about my mother," an octogenarian woman confided to me some years ago. Her mother had been dead for forty years but, still, her words were punctuated with a sigh and she is not a woman given to sighs. The "sigh" was full to bursting with angst, regret, love and admiration. But to tell you the truth, I've had it up to here with all of that. Angst gives me gas and crying leaves me with a headache. Oh, I, too, have had my fair share of maternally induced distress. But life is too short to wallow in it. My mother would not have approved. She would have said that it's part of the job. Now, I'm a mother and a grand-mother, leaving angst, tears, regrets and other maternally induced mayhem in *my* wake. (Actually, it's rather fun but that's material for another essay.) I'm here to write a letter to my mother, the collector.

Some background: my mother loved to collect...things, just as

Sesame Street's Count loves to count. By reality TV standards, some might be tempted to use the word "hoarder" to describe her hobby, but Mom wouldn't have qualified. Her acquisitions were meticulously researched and carefully chosen. Each item, whether jewelry, dish or artist's sketch, was appropriately displayed, stored or preserved. Unlike the television programs, filth and cats never entered into the equation. Lastly, Mom went through phases: Depression glass one year, turquoise Southwest jewelry the next, then art, vintage books. Once a new muse infected her imagination, she selected a collection for retirement to be gently gathered, then sold or bartered away. Her condo was simply not spacious enough to house all of the treasures she loved.

Or so we thought.

"Now remember, girls," she told my sister and me during a holiday visit. "If anything happens to me…" Claire and I would groan at this point. Our mother was indestructible. "There's no need to squabble over the china." *As if we would…* my sister's expression said. "There are six sets in the basement." *Six* sets? After she died in 2004, we found out that she had ten.

Dene, her seventy-nine-year-old sister, grumbled as we sorted through the china, Mom's living room floor covered with boxes, newspaper and towers of dinner, salad, and dessert plates, bowls, serving dishes, cups and saucers. Did I mention the one-of-a-kind butter dish? The four meat platters? The pineapple patterned sherbets?

"I plan to have a chat with your mother when I get to the pearly gates," Aunt Dene said sternly, staring into the abyss of yet another box—this time, it was Christmas china. "This is ridiculous."

The china and other collections were my inheritance—mine and my sister's. Ten sets of china (actually, it was twelve, I forgot about the ones with the silver border), a mini-gallery of art, uncountable pieces of jewelry (Mom's real passion). Every room in my home contains some item of my mother's. I rarely go out without wearing at least one piece of her jewelry. Surrounding myself with items from Mom's various collections helped me cope with the loss when she was gone. But as Mother's Day, 2004 approached, my first Mother's Day without her, the art, the table settings, and the jewelry fell short. The comfort they initially afforded dissipated like a puff of smoke and left me feeling like an orphan. Being a mother was not enough. I felt that I needed to *have* a mother in order to get through this most Hallmark of holidays.

You have to understand, from the time that I was small, Mother's Day was a big deal celebrated in our home along the lines of a Broadway show with cast, sets, props and, on at least one occasion, music. Dad set the tone (he was both producer and director.) My family made the holiday a real photo-op-worthy event: breakfast-in-bed, flowers, dinner and cards, both hand-made and otherwise. We planned for weeks in advance, schemed and orchestrated the one-woman holiday from sun-up (always way too early for my mother, but she was a good sport) to sundown and dinner, Dad's domain, oddly composed but nutritious. The kitchen was a wreck when the festivities were over and at least one minor disaster was inevitable (one year, the oven overheated and smoked), but Mom never failed to express surprise and gratitude. Even as adults, Mother's Day was serious business. A flurry of phone calls, emails and text messages flew between Cincinnati and Chicago.

"Did you order the flowers?"

"Yep. TTYL."

"Sent card yesterday. Have you talked with her?"

"Did you sign my name?"

"Oh, @#$% !"

And then the big day arrived and we each called her—early—because Mom never let grass grow under her feet. She was either getting ready to go somewhere or had just returned. My fingers still itch when I think about those Sunday morning calls. I remember her phone number with perfect clarity. I think I always will. But in 2004, the Grinch stole Mother's Day from me.

And then, just like the Grinch, an epiphany. There was another collection of Mom's that I had overlooked, one that was not bubble-wrapped or stored in a fifteen-gallon plastic tub. Nor would it appear in black and white on a probate court estate inventory. I could not fathom a Mother's Day without sending a Mother's Day card. And so, I sent Mother's Day *cards* instead. I sent them to her friends. These women constituted yet another collection lovingly curated and cherished by my mother and bequeathed to me, along with the zebra-print coffee mugs, half-pound-weight turquoise cuff bracelet and Warhol scarf. I realized that one of my mother's greatest legacies to me was the gift of her friends, women whom had known her well. The words that follow are a gift of gratitude to my mother, Myrtle Jones Humphrey, and to her friends, her living legacy, women whom have illuminated my path over the past few years just by being there.

Dear Mom,

I'll keep this short because I know that, wherever you are, you are busy.

I'd like to think that you would be proud of me. I am hard-headed, dreamy and oblivious a lot of the time, but your advice to me has been invaluable. The first Mother's Day without you, I was totally prepared to wallow in grief, tears and tissues. And wear black a lot, something I'm sure that you would have approved of. The black, I mean. Being a fan of Edgar Allan Poe's, I adore unrequited grief, as you know. But your words rang in my ears, words you spoke after the death of your husband: "You can't make a career out of mourning." So I sighed (I've become very good at sighing), blew my nose, put the tissues away and took myself off to the card store to buy Mother's Day cards for your girlfriends. Wearing black, of course—you always said it was chic. Anyway, I'll have you know that I spent a respectable amount of time and money. I didn't skimp. Each card was chosen to fit the woman to whom it would be sent. And, following your cues, I added a hand-written message to each one: How are you feeling? To an aunt who'd had surgery; where are you going next? To a globe-trotting pal and so on. But as I scribbled away, a tiny thought took root in my head. What is a friend? What is the nature of friendship and how does it nurture us? I drove home pondering these questions. I am pretty sure that you had this in mind all along. Friendship was always very important to you.

The women who would receive these cards were hand-picked. They were your pals, partners-in-crime and BFFs (to use today's vernacular). They had not only accessorized your life with love, laughter, empathy and companionship, but they were also reflections of your interests, your experiences and your memories. Of course I didn't forget your sisters Dene and Hattie, (FYI: Mom, Aunt Dene's still ticked off about the Depression glass collection that we discovered in a box at the back of the basement in the corner behind the furnace filters...), your cousin, the amazing Dorothy (if it's quiet where you are, it's because she's ninety-seven this year) and "Aunt" Carol, who's recently reminded me that she grew up with you and remembers when...never mind. I sent cards to your girlfriends, all of them "true blue"—a phrase you liked to use. It means to be trusted, honest and loyal.

I realized practically the moment that I dropped the envelopes into the mailbox that these women reflected the clubs you enjoyed, the trips that you took, the music, art and jewelry that you surrounded your life with and the memories you cherished. They had been tested by time, laughter and tears—they had been vetted and not found wanting. And, I was startled to realize, they had been bequeathed to me.

Why had I been feeling sorry for myself? There was a chest of riches right at my feet.

I wasn't an orphan at all—I had all of these mothers to support, guide and look after me; wise women who were counselors, nurturing me into the next act of my life. They gave me the benefit of their own experience and, sometimes, they spoke with your voice, knowing instinctively because they had known you, what to say. All my mothers, scolding me, bossing me around, reminding me, praising me, supporting me, taking the baton from you and guiding me along with the beacon from its light, because, well, because that was their job now, just as it was in our old neighborhood when I was ten. Every mother in Eastgate was my mother.

And so, thanks to Aunt Carol who grew up with you on Fourth Street and Cousin Dorothy, who remembers "how it was" and reminds me. Thanks to Nikki for firm but gentle advice, to dear Lena for getting tough with me about the realities of life and death and getting older ("Get on with it!"), to Aunts Dene and Hattie, to LaVerne (you two fiends traded the most outrageous birthday cards every year in July, the month of your mutual birthdays), to dear Shirley "Mary" who misses your chats, to my godmother, Joan, to all of your fabulous friends and to you, Mom—thank you.

I whispered my thanks to you for your innumerable gifts to me many times in the hospital room. I will never know if you heard me. There is so much that I owe you. There is so much to thank you for, more than I can remember. But before I forget (again), thank you for granting me the gift of your friends—they were the treasures of your heart and now they are the treasures of mine.

Post-script: Thanks for the giraffe-patterned dessert plates, too.

Sheila L. Williams sees herself as an old-fashioned storyteller. "Storytelling is as old as campfires, maybe older. For me and for those like me, telling stories is part of our DNA." Sheila is the author of four novels, including Dancing on the Edge of the Roof *(which has been optioned for film by Alfre Woodard) and* Girls Most Likely. *She has taught creative writing for UCLA Extension. Sheila lives in northern Kentucky with her family.*

Playing Favorites
Sofia Quintero

Dear Abuela,

Every time Carmen says I look just like you, the irony hits me like a gnat sting between the eyes. After all, she's your namesake, and me? We never had a meaningful relationship.

My most indelible memories of you from childhood aren't the things that people usually recall when they speak of their grandmothers. Certain words ring in my head. *Pendeja. Puñeta.* Even *pata* just because whenever Natalie would come to visit, we'd hide out in your bathroom to gossip away from adult ears. You would pound on the door and yell at us to get out, suggesting that we were doing something untoward.

Looking back I realize that it was more than being only a year apart that bonded Carmen's younger sister and me. I don't think Nat and I ever named—at least not as little girls—what we shared. That was the knowledge that among the granddaughters, we were not favored. This awareness included the undeniably possible reasons why you would never dote on us the way you did Carmen or Magda and then later, Melissa or Krystal.

Our Spanish was too weak.

Our eyes were too brown.

Our skin too dark, our hair too curly.

Perhaps you might've overlooked one of these traits—Carmen is no more or less Afro-Latina than either of us. We could not, however, possess all these characteristics and expect you to take us shopping or remember our birthdays. Here at the age of forty-three, I sit here embarrassed as I write this to you for no other reason than I can only do so in English.

And yet today almost no one in the family can look at a picture of me with glasses and a blowout and not see you.

I often regale my friends with tales of your outlandishness, disrupting their anecdotes of sweet *abuelitas* who fit the traditional profile. They talk about the refuge that was their grandmother's home, a haven for conspiracies kept from disciplinarian parents, repositories of affirmations and spoils, a garden of lessons from the sensual to the pragmatic. Then my turn comes, and I quip, "I learned how to curse in Spanish from my grandmother." I pause for effect, then add, "Because she was hurling those words at me." And once I had their gasping attention, I'd follow with a second-hand story that exemplified your tart tongue and brassy behavior—my favorites being the ones that involved Ma and you butting heads.

Something shifted when I became a teenager, and I wonder if maybe you began to see yourself in me. I remember the day you called me to come over to your house. It was the day after my fifteenth birthday. *La quince* is a significant birthday for a Latina unless, of course, she's very *Americana* like me. Even if my parents could have afforded it, I wouldn't have wanted a *quinceañera*. As much as I crushed on boys, the affair seemed too much like a *boda*, and I had long decided there'd be no weddings or children until after I graduated college. I already knew that if there was any money to spare, it had to go to my education.

So I thought nothing of your summoning. I just figured you wanted me to come over to pick up some homemade *arroz con dulce* or *flan* for my family. The Quinteros may not have been your favorites, but you did think of us at times. I suspect now that you thought of us more often than you showed. Or maybe that's just what I want to believe now that you're gone.

When I arrived I lingered in the dining area, cooing in front of Cuca's cage hoping to get her to speak to me. You called me into the bedroom, and I found you standing before the dresser and holding something behind your back. In Spanish you wished me a happy birthday, asked God to bless me and held out a red velvet jewelry box. It flit across my mind that someone—probably Ma with that unmistakable haughtiness—brought the oversight to your attention once the day had come and gone without acknowledgment from you. Still I was moved that you had thought to do something for this critical milestone. That you didn't resort to buying a card and stuffing a bill in it like you had in the past. Like you had when you remembered.

Inside the box was a gold herringbone chain that hung into a V-shape. I immediately put it on and skipped the two blocks home to show Ma. Even she had to smile. I didn't take off that necklace for years even when it clashed with everything else I was wearing. You can see it in my high school graduation picture. My college graduation portrait, too. I only stopped wearing it when the V became so worn from my constant fiddling, I feared that the links would break, and I would lose it. I now keep the chain tucked away. I'll probably never wear it again, but I won't give it up, either.

Once I became an adult, our relationship lost tension without gaining intimacy. We were cordial but never close. It seemed like we both resigned ourselves that this was the best we could do. Sometimes I wondered if you ever looked at me across your table at Thanksgiving and Christmas and regretted not having invested more time in building a relationship with me. Didn't I grow up to be a grandmother's dream? But you couldn't brag about me to the other ladies at St. Joan's if you didn't know what to say.

When you passed, the bulk of my sadness was sympathy for the relatives who were closer or otherwise emotionally enmeshed with you. You were neither the worst nor the best to me, and so there was an emotional cancelling out that only allowed me to feel by proxy. I hurt for Carmen who essentially was your daughter by bond if not by birth. I took pride in my father, the oldest son who cared for you in your final days instead of using your favoritism as an excuse to abrogate responsibility. I forgave for Ma and cousin Natalie who were at your bedside at home when you passed, allowing them the closure they desperately needed.

I thought we were done, but lately I've been dreaming consistently of you. My experience with breast cancer has catalyzed deep emotional healing that these dreams tell me is only beginning. Rewriting my personal myth involves uncovering the mythology I might have inherited from my immediate ancestors even if only by intuition. You were the only biological grandparent I had ever known, and so as I embarked on this excavation, I presumed my focus had to be on the three who died while my parents were still young children. Yet what immediately became evident was that my journey to wholeness requires that I discover and accept the ways that I am indeed your granddaughter, good, bad or indifferent, from psychic wound to ancient strength passed down through Ramirez DNA.

Now I accept that I could have made the choice to do more to get to know you, and that as we both grew older, you would have welcomed my efforts. I can see that now, especially when I recall how the thaw melted between Ma and you when you chose to mother her during a crisis. I could have sat in your kitchen and asked you to tell me your stories—oh, how you would've obliged! They were my stories, too, but now the language for them for which I have the most facility—the language of words—is gone with you. I may be able to access them through the feelings and images embedded in cellular memory, but you're meeting me more than halfway through my dreams.

All I can do now is forgive myself for not missing what I never had while I still had time to cultivate it.

From where you are I bet you clearly see how I inherited much more than your appearance. For years I wrongfully attributed certain traits—my eagerness to say the unsaid, my more than occasionally bawdy humor, my interminable sense of entitlement and willingness to fight for things women of color are not supposed to dare want, never mind have, do and be—to Ma. Now I can see how many of them, despite our distance, you somehow managed to will to me. And I'm grateful, *'uela*. Thank you.

Wherever you are, I know that you're at peace and so I should be, too. That you watch over me, your "looksake," as you do all your forebears, intervening on my behalf with God probably more often than polite. And that you no longer play favorites.

Con mucho amor siempre,
La Sofía

Sofia Quintero is a cultural activist who has written five novels and twice as many short stories and novellas across genres for virtually every major publishing house. When not working as a teaching artist for the National Book Foundation and Urban Word NYC, she's finishing her second YA novel, Show and Prove, *which will be published by Knopf in 2014.*

Once I Had a Mother
Deepa Agarwal

Mothers are worshipped in my country. A girl's mother is supposed to be her ideal, the person who provides a hallowed role model, handed down over generations, for her to follow. This is where my problem began—my mother did not subscribe to this role model. Ignoring cultural norms, she never attempted to embrace the role of domestic goddess and grand martyr—considered an essential component of Indian womanhood. Shockingly, she hardly ever entered the kitchen, even to supervise the cook or bothered with the dusting. My father managed the household details—sending for groceries, keeping accounts. As a result, I grew up surrounded by a cloud of whispered criticism. In time her deficiencies as a woman overpowered me so that I vowed never to be like her.

Many years later I realized what a big mistake I'd made when I decided to be everything Mummy was not, just to get approval from the world at large. When I got married, I blithely gave up my job. I felt I had to, in order to transform into an exemplary homemaker, wife, mother and daughter-in-law. How could I have anticipated that I was not cut out for this part? Attempting to cook perfect meals day in and day out and pampering relatives did not, alas, provide the fulfillment I had believed it would. And being financially dependent began to chip away at my self-esteem. After a while a grudging admiration for my mother grew in my heart. Despite pressure from her elders, she had never given up her teaching job. It proved to be the wisest decision she made. When my father died without much money in the bank, at least she had a small salary and later her pension to sustain her. Yes, Mummy had been much smarter than I thought she was.

There was also a myth prevalent in my extended family that she was a helpless kind of person, unable to manage her own affairs. It was true to some extent. She was not someone who could undertake the responsibility of supervising home repairs, for instance. All the same, when my children were growing up, my mother provided the emotional backing I needed at the time. She lived in my hometown, far from the distant city of Delhi where I had settled. But each summer I spent at least a month with her. It was the perfect holiday. The children were taken care of and I didn't have to stress about running the house efficiently. In winter she would visit me, often bringing domestic help along to ease my routine.

The last two years of my mother's life were painful. She suffered from pulmonary fibrosis, a progressive disease that deprived her body of oxygen. Eventually even the oxygen machine was not effective. Sadly, she was with my youngest brother at the time and I didn't have the opportunity to say goodbye in person. This is just one more in the list of my regrets connected with my relationship with my mother.

Dearest Mummy,
Some years ago I found the last letter you wrote to me in a pile of old papers. One sentence was repeated over and over again—"You haven't written to me, I feel very lonely."
How ironic it is that twenty-four years after you left us, I am

writing this letter, considering I was so irregular when you were alive! But all these years there has been plenty of time to think about you, to brood over the fact that I could not offer you the unconditional love that I gave Papa.

I must confess that this bothered me even when you were alive. Because aren't children are supposed to love their parents unquestioningly? That's the rule in Indian families, part of those traditional values etched in stone. For me to admit this feels sacrilegious.

There was indeed a time when my affection for you was unequivocal. As a small girl, I remember how happily I would run to greet you when you returned home at the end of a school day, carrying a small brown paper bag of treats—the laddoos I loved or a slab of chocolate. I don't know when I began to be uncomfortably aware that you were not the perfect person I wanted my mother to be, and a grievance took root. I have to admit that I was looking at you through the fractured prism of other eyes, of people who could not accept you for what you were. People who somewhere resented the fact you never made an attempt to fit into the accepted mold.

When Papa died, one of your senior colleagues made a remark that really stung me. She said, "Your father pampered her like a child; now it is your job to do the same." I was twenty years old and these words infuriated me. How could she suggest we reverse our roles? It was perhaps understandable that Papa treated you like a child. He was eighteen years older than you and fortunately not the conventional kind of husband who expects his wife to wait on him hand and foot. You had health problems and he loved you enough to take you as you were. Perhaps he understood your insecurities, too, and the circumstances that created them.

This is what I have been thinking about for the past several years. Trying to understand what it meant to be you—a child who lost both her parents by the age of nine and was brought up by a bachelor brother. And how the fact that he had joined the freedom movement against British rule and was often in jail made it more complicated for you. By the time you reached your early twenties, he, too, was gone and you had to struggle to survive on your own.

Blinded by the image we create of them, we often can't look upon our parents as ordinary humans, with scars and traumas. As our nurturers and protectors, we expect them to be super strong, and resent any signs of weakness. Whenever Papa fell ill, tears would stream down your face. I hated it, hated that you were always so anxious and made up my mind I would never be like that.

Indeed I have tried to be strong in the face of adversity. After Papa died, as your eldest child, I attempted to provide you whatever companionship I could. But I am painfully conscious that it was not as wholehearted as it should have been. It was much, much later that realization came, that it was not just you leaning on me. You propped me up as much—if not more. The most telling fact was that your love always remained unconditional. It was I who returned to being the pampered child when I spent my summers with you, and went back with renewed strength to grapple with the everyday problems that sometimes felt insurmountable.

When you passed away, it took a while to register what had gone from my life. There was no one to fuss over me, to worry that I was wearing myself out, or not eating enough. No more letters demanding my attention, but also no reliving my childhood. The parental house was emptied out and only the fading perfume of memories remained.

But by then I had begun to unwind the coils of the web I had spun around myself. Remembering you, I was assuring myself that it was not wrong to make my own choices. That I didn't have to dutifully squeeze into the image that had been created for the being known as "woman"—the silent, uncomplaining drudge, content to remain confined within the walls of home, to glean a meager joy from what was doled out to her. I was learning to do things that pleased me rather than force myself to do those that I hoped would please others.

Now I was beginning to appreciate the person you had the courage to be, to grasp that, however fragile or childlike you may have appeared, you were actually quite revolutionary.

Thank you, Mummy, for being yourself, despite all the pressures to conform, for showing me that it is possible to survive outside the safe bounds of tradition. It took me time to blast away the fog that obscured my real role model. But how grateful I am, eventually I could find the way home.

Deepa Agarwal writes fiction and poetry for both children and adults and has over fifty books published. She received the National Award for Children's Literature for her picture book, Ashok's New Friends, *while her historical fiction,* Caravan to Tibet, *was on the IBBY (International Board on Books for Young People) Honor List 2008. Her work has been translated into several Indian and foreign languages. She also translates from Hindi, her mother tongue, into English and has received fellowships to research children's literature.*

GET YOUR OWN DUNGEON!
And Other Francesisms That Used to Work My Last Nerve

Tracy Price-Thompson

The project hallway was hot as all get out as I stood in front of the fifth-floor apartment and tried to pull my shit together. The block party had been live, and once again I had missed my curfew.

I stared at the nameplate on the door, then smoothed my hair down and patted my face with the edge of my T-shirt. I had friends who could walk up in their mama's house at any time of night looking any old kind of way, but when I crossed the threshold of apartment 5-G, I knew my act had better be correct.

The joint I'd smoked had my eyes red and my mouth bone-dry, but when that door swung open, it was the slender, butterscotch-colored woman with the reddish-brown hair who had me sweating bullets and my heart pumping Kool-Aid.

Right away I knew I was in *trouble*. Hell hath no fury like a pissed-off Frances with one hand on her hip and an extension cord dangling from the other one.

The fire in her flashing brown eyes said it all, but of course her mouth just had to go ahead and say it, too.

"You must think you're grown, huh?"

Hell yeah.

It was two months after my sixteenth birthday and all my best friends were pregnant.

"No. I don't think I'm grown."

"Oh yes you do. What time did I tell you to be in here?"

"Ten."

"And what time is it now?"

I had the nerve to shrug. Like she wouldn't knock me straight into the middle of next week.

"Eleven."

"Let me tell you something, Tracy. This is *my* house, and you're not gonna prance in here whenever you get ready. I told you to be in here at ten, and that's exactly what I meant. *Ten.* Did you read the name on the door before you came in? It said, '*F. Carr*' and that's *me.* Now, if you're too grown to follow my rules, then you'd better get your *own* damn dungeon! It ain't gotta be a mansion, and it ain't gotta be a castle, either. It can be a *dungeon*, baby, just as long as it's *yours!*"

"But I was right downstairs on the porch with so-and-so! Her mother let her stay out—"

"I don't care *what* so-and so's mother let her do! So-and-so's mama pays the rent upstairs, and I pay the rent *down here*, and as long as you're living here with me, you're gonna do what *I* tell you to do!"

And then she said it: "Get in that room and get undressed. I ain't beating my clothes, baby. Uh-uh. I ain't hardly beating my clothes!"

I walked into my bedroom and got ready to strip. My mother didn't play. She said what she meant, and she meant what the hell she said. There were two things her children could count on from her: one was loyalty and the other was consistency. She was a straight-shooter and her word was her bond. If she told you not to do something, then she meant not to dammit *do it*, and if you were bad enough to disobey her, then you'd better be bad enough to take what you had coming.

And what I had coming that hot summer night was a good-old-fashioned ass-whipping.

It wasn't the first one, and it wouldn't be the last one, either.

Don't get me wrong, I was my mother's baby girl. Her love child. I had her entire heart in my hand, and we were tighter than tight. But that didn't stop her from doing her job. All that love she had for me didn't stop her from swinging a belt when she needed to. It didn't stop her from being the brick wall that I pushed against, or from demanding that I live up to my potential and do great things with my life.

My mother was selfless when it came to her children, and she always put us first. My father was an electrical engineer and she was a nurse. My parents were like Saturday night and Sunday morning, but they were also best friends. They respected each other and banded together in a united front when it came to raising us kids. They were educated professionals and I felt privileged to belong to them. My siblings and I were well-fed and well-clothed. We lived *in* the projects, but we weren't *of* the projects. It was where we were at the time, but not where we were striving to always be. Eddie and Frances had a broader vision for us. Big hopes and even bigger dreams.

As a stylish Sagittarian, my mother was always the life of the party. Physically beautiful, fashionable, and outgoing, she was a beacon of sunshine in the projects. She loved and nurtured everyone around her, and people flocked toward her light in droves. She was a nurse who stitched up cuts for the neighborhood boys. She pierced ears, bandaged bruises, fed the hungry, and loaned out plenty of money. And she made sure every dime of it got paid back, too.

She was well-known and respected in our neighborhood. Well-loved by many.

But in the summer of 1979, I couldn't stand her.

For some reason, the mother that I'd always been so close to, the gorgeous woman who had babied me and made me feel special my whole life had turned on me. She'd been breathing fire down my neck for months, watching me like a hawk. I was a Brooklyn girl, and I liked the streets. There was always something exciting going on in my neighborhood. Boys, music, parties, weed. I lived on a huge block that held eight tall project buildings. Each building had sixteen floors, and each floor had eight apartments. We were a large community, full of wild thangs. And we were surrounded by other blocks and project buildings that were just as big and wild as we were.

Like most of the kids in my building, I was used to having a certain amount of freedom to roam. After all, there were no cell phones, iPads, or Facebook back in those days, so putting on some cute clothes and hanging out on the block was how we did our social networking.

But in the summer of 1979 my mother put the brakes on all that. She had a funky attitude with me for no reason at all. She was constantly crowding me, up in my face questioning my every move, dominating me, sniffing me out like a bloodhound, watching me like a rat on a piece of cheese. Tightening my net.

She made it crystal-clear that *she* was the chief bitch on the scene. She let it be known that her will, and the strength of her character, were far stronger than and superior to mine. She told me right to my face that she had brought me into this world and she wouldn't hesitate to take me out.

Fear God, and fear Mama!

"Just *try me*, Tracy," she'd growl with her fists balled up when I sucked my teeth under my breath or rolled my eyes behind her back. "You just try me, *okay?*" And then she'd point down at the kitchen floor that was covered in a pattern of blue, green, and silver linoleum and promise, "Because if you do, there'll be a lump in this floor where I *bury* your ass!"

Goodness gracious! Did she really mean all that?

Hell yeah!

Was all of that beat-ass talk just her way of trying to scare me straight?

Hell no!

Even as a sixteen-year-old project girl, there were certain things I knew for sure: There was a God up above, I had a nose on my face, the sun rose in the East and set in the West, and if I stuck one toe across the line, my mother would kill me and gladly go to jail.

But I wanted to do what *I* wanted to do, and I was getting tired of hearing that crazy stuff Frances talked. If she was trying to impress me with her hard-earned knowledge, it wasn't working.

"Someday you're going to look down and see my hand coming out of your sleeve," she once told me.

And if I do, I'd thought, *I'm gonna chop that sucker right off!*

Sometimes her countless little sayings and cautionary anecdotes seemed downright ridiculous.

Get your own dungeon! she loved to tell me.

I'm not one of your friends in the street, you hear me?

Birds of a feather flock together! You are judged by the company you keep!

Nothing beats a failure but a try!

Wherever you tear your drawers, that's where I'm gonna cut your ass!

Every shut eye ain't sleep, and every goodbye ain't gone!

If you lie, you'll steal! There's nothing worse than a liar except a thief!

A hard head makes a soft behind!

I punish you because I love you.

Get up, girl! Nobody's gonna drag you through life! Learn how to start your own engine!

Oh, so you did something wrong and you knew you were doing wrong? Well, don't think you're gonna hide behind me. Get on over there and take your licks, baby!

I don't care where so-and-so is going or what so-and-so got permission to do! YOU'RE not going! If so-and-so, jumps off the roof are you gonna jump off with them?

You'd better make your bed the way you want to lay in it, baby. If you make it hard, you'll lay in it hard. If you make it soft, you can lay in it soft.

Be your own woman and stand on your own two feet!

I'm not gonna be here forever, Tracy. One day—it could be today or it could be tomorrow—but one day I'm gonna close my eyes, you know...

Goodness! My mother blabbed all those old sayings so many times that I knew them all by heart. I used to move my lips and recite all that crazy stuff with her, mocking her, matching her pace and inflections to a tee. I'd get behind her back and imitate her. The way her hand rested on her poked-out hip. The sassy smirk of her lips. The fire and the grit in her eyes. Hell, I knew what Frances Carr was going to say before the words were even out of her mouth!

It was a good while before I realized why my mother had been so hard on me during that hot summer of 1979. By the time I understood exactly why she had harassed me and ridden me so hard and how, with her motherly wrath and wisdom she had saved my life, I was already a wife and a mother myself.

After all, I had just turned sixteen that summer and all of my best friends were pregnant.

And all but one of them was younger than I was.

"Try me, Tracy. Just try me. You hear?"

I was a tough teenager. A real project girl. Hardheaded. Sneaky. Slick. I liked hanging out. I liked doing what everybody else was doing. Whatever my friends did, I did it, too. Sometimes I did it first.

"There'll be a lump in this floor where I bury your ass!"

I was respectful inside the house, but I went for bad outside. I talked a lot of trash and I could back it up, too.

Water seeks its own level!

Once, I played hooky from school with some of my girls from the building. We rode the subway to South Shore High School, back in the day where the neighborhood was all white. We were broke and hungry as we walked around the residential area outside the school, and we joked about knocking an old white lady down and snatching her pocketbook so we could buy a slice of pizza.

One of us wasn't joking.

You are judged by the company you keep!

But I was Frances's child. I could never get that broke. Or that hungry.

My mother would have killed me. And gladly gone to jail.

Yeah, I went for bad with my Brooklyn self, but my mother really *was* bad.

Frances had an arsenal of weapons to back her up, too. Standards and expectations. Extension cords and leather belts. House shoes, brooms, and frying pans.

It was all because of her that I graduated from high school less than a month after my seventeenth birthday, a whole year ahead of my class.

And it was Frances's fault that I went to college and graduated with a bachelor's degree and a master's degree, too.

It was due to all that heat Frances breathed down my neck that I never snatched an old lady's purse and I never got arrested.

Because it was Frances who had brought me into this world, and Frances who would've surely taken me out.

Make no mistake, my mother would have killed me. And gladly gone to jail.

But she would have taken a bullet for me, too.

She would have stood up to a grizzly bear for me. She would have stared down a lion. Swallowed an ocean full of salty water. Rushed into a burning building. Wrestled with an alligator. Jumped into a raging river full of hungry piranhas. For me. For me! For *me*.

Because as a mother, *that* was her job, too.

Many years ago, when I was a young soldier raising a family of my own in Germany, I sent my mother a card. It was out of the blue, and there was no particular reason for it. It wasn't her birthday or Mother's Day, or any special occasion at all.

It was a handwritten thank-you card. Just to show my appreciation for the job she had done all those years ago, and the job she was still doing as she continued to parent me at every opportunity, even though by then I was grown and on my own.

I thanked my mother for the small things she'd done, like giving me a bath when I was a child, and putting me to bed in clean pajamas between a top sheet *and* a bottom sheet every night. I thanked her for being careful when she cut my toenails and gentle when she stuck a Q-tip in my ears.

I thanked her for providing me with a strong sense of security, and the knowledge that I was loved and would always be safe and protected. I thanked her for her caring hand of comfort on my forehead and her hot bowl of tenderness and chicken soup whenever I was sick.

I thanked Frances for knowing when to back me down and intimidate me, and when to let me be. For knowing when to whip my behind, and when to kiss away my tears. For knowing when to jump between me and a hot stove, and when to let my hard head make my behind nice and soft.

I thanked her for rushing to my defense in an argument—but only when I was right. When I was wrong, she'd look dead at me and say, "Tracy, you are *wrong*," and I thanked her for that, too.

I gave my mother thanks for raising me to be loyal to my siblings. She made it clear that friends were for sometimes, but family was forever. She told my sisters and me that someday we would need each other, and she was absolutely right.

I thanked her for making my babies *her* babies. I thanked her for taking care of them when I was deployed with the military, and for loving them and disciplining them the same as she'd done for me.

I thanked my mother for standing her ground in her house, and for teaching me that her dungeon belong to *her*, and I could either get with the program and respect it, or get out there and get my own.

I thanked her for instilling fear in me. The fear of God and the fear of Mama, too. Sometimes that fear was the only thing that stood between me and a fatal mistake.

I thanked her for making "lazy" a four-letter word, and the worst possible insult that anyone could ever hurl at you. Because of her I have never tolerated or respected laziness. In myself, or in other people.

I thanked her for demanding excellence, and for refusing to put her foot in my back and prop me up. She was wise enough to know that if I relied on her to push me through life, I'd never learn how to start my own engine.

I thanked Frances for having strict rules and for dealing out swift punishment. She taught me to discipline myself so that others didn't have to, and instilled in me the certainty that there would always be consequences and repercussions for my actions.

I thanked her for having high expectations of me, and for requiring me to work hard and live up to my full potential. I was a silly, hardheaded young girl and you couldn't tell me much of anything.

If she had yielded or surrendered just one inch of ground, I would have overflowed just like water, seeking my lowest level.

I thanked her for being my rock of support when I was in need, and my soft spot to land on when my ass hit the ground. But only temporarily. She was smart enough to let me rest for a minute and catch my breath, and then push me back out of the nest, back into the world, and demand that I fly.

I thanked my mother for never telling anyone about the shameful thing I did that one time. I thanked her for not throwing it up in my face, even when she had every right to. I thanked her for understanding me, and for keeping my secrets, and for being loyal to me with her whole heart, even through my many faults.

I thanked my mother for loving me so wisely and so thoroughly. Especially during those hot summer days of 1979 when I couldn't stand her.

Because my mother knew that one day she'd close her eyes and leave this world, and I would be left to stand on my own two feet.

She knew I'd be left to start my own engine and to get my own dungeon.

Recently, my sister, Michelle, and I were going through some of my mother's belongings. There were countless old photos, report cards from elementary school, immunization records from the health station, and yes, lots and lots of cards.

One card in particular caught my eye, and when I opened it, I smiled. I read all the way down to the last line before my breath caught in my throat.

"Thank you, Mommy," I'd written all those years ago, "If I can do half as good with my kids as you did with me, then I'll be happy."

That wasn't the last thank-you that I ever offered my mother. No, the final thank-you came seventeen years ago at her funeral.

Although her death had been sudden and unexpected and I was

devastated by my loss, the one thing that I could hold on to was the fact that as her daughter, I had no regrets. Not a single one. There had been nothing except love, affection, and intense appreciation between us. She had been the best mother in the world, and I had been her grateful baby girl. We had spoiled and favored each other. We had kissed and hugged. We had laughed together and cried together. And at the moment of her death there was nothing left unsaid between us because from the time I could talk, the words *I love you* had been exchanged from our mouths, our hearts, and our souls at least ten billion times.

Thank you, Mommy. Thank you for every single thing.

I miss my mother. I miss her smile, her laughter, her wisdom and her guidance. I miss the protection of her arms. I miss having someone in my life who loves me enough to kill me.

I thank God for Frances Carr. She was one hell of a woman. She was loving, and she was affectionate. She was funny, and she was loyal. She was wise, and she was strong. She was hard, and she was fair.

She laughed and she joked, but she didn't play.

She was good to me.

She was better than she had to be.

Of course she was. She was my mother.

Tracy Price-Thompson is the national bestselling author of Black Coffee, Chocolate Sangria, Knockin' Boots, Gather Together in My Name, 1-900-Anytime, *and the 2005 Hurston/Wright Legacy Award Winner,* A Woman's Worth. *She is a retired U.S. Army engineer officer and lives with her husband, Gregory, in the Bay Area.*

MAMA
Carol Taylor

"I do not sit down at my desk to put into verse something that is already clear in my mind. If it were clear in my mind, I should have no incentive or need to write about it. We do not write in order to be understood; we write in order to understand." —C.S. LEWIS

I lost my mother to Alzheimer's and dementia in July 2011 after being her caregiver for five years; she was sixty-seven years old. Even though ours was a tumultuous relationship taking care of her fell to me, the youngest, because I was the only one of her four children who didn't run away from it...who could handle it. But I couldn't handle it; I just couldn't run away from it.

Even after her death, I still grapple with the same feelings I had during the five years I took care of her: ambivalence, rage, sadness, fear, apathy and regret. With my father's death my mother was now free from his overbearing, domineering and tyrannical hold on her, but I never got the opportunity to talk to her about the things I'd struggled with my entire childhood and much of my adulthood. My throat is choked with all the things I didn't get the chance to say because my mother had passed on to a different place mentally long before she passed on physically. It was so like her to get the last word.

In America, Canada and England, many West Indians grow up in houses filled with pseudo-French Provincial furniture wrapped up tightly in a protective plastic skin that clings to the body in summer like a hot sweaty embrace. West Indians love to live in a faux world: Faux mahogany dining sets nestled comfortably in retro Edwardian living rooms. Implausible ornaments crowded ten to a side table. Elaborate wicker displays and monumental fake flower arrangements. And wall-to-wall carpeting protected by plastic runners, crisscrossing every possible walkway.

In my West Indian family, I was definitely the apple that had fallen far from the tree. Actually, I'd fallen and rolled all the way down the hill.

For me plastic was for storing food not furniture. Inconceivably, I was born a minimalist into a family of ceramic figurine collectors. My childhood bedroom, incongruous in my family's overstuffed home, was a monastic, whitewashed space with the walls embellished only by the black and white Ansel Adams photographs I'd cut out from a wall calendar. My wooden floor, polished to a high sheen, was a natural oasis in a world of wall-to-wall. I lived "less is more" long before I knew whom to attribute the quote to: I as eight years old.

I was as different from my family as night is from day. I went away to college when my siblings opted to stay close to home. I traveled and lived abroad when my family thought Miami was an international trip. I chose not to marry when my siblings were pairing off with their childhood sweethearts getting married and starting families.

So imagine my surprise when after my father died suddenly from a heart attack at just sixty-five, and my mother succumbed to Alzheimer's and dementia, I, the wayward child, somehow became her caregiver. Mind you, I didn't volunteer, I didn't even think I'd be in the running. I'm the youngest, the brashest, "the most likely to..." Yet somehow my siblings decided I was the one for the job. They were right, I *was*. If only because I was the only one who didn't, couldn't push it off, who didn't, couldn't run away from it... This letter to my mother encapsulates all the things I wish I'd been able to say, and some things I probably shouldn't.

Mama,

Let me be clear here: You are the reason I never married or had children and because of this, we have unfinished business that even your death has not settled. It's been two years since you passed; yet your ashes sit in the box they arrived in, on a shelf in my bedroom closet. I'm tasked with sprinkling them in the ocean so you can find your way back home to Jamaica and to your husband, my father, whose ashes you and I sprinkled into the Atlantic five years earlier.

For once I have the upper hand, as you rest neatly packed into a box no bigger than a breadbox not more than three feet from where I rest my own head. I can say anything I want and you have to listen. I can say all the things I've been meaning to tell you, about your emotionally and physically abusive marriage, and your emotional and physical abuse of your children because of your emotionally and physically abusive marriage.

I never understood why you traded your mother's abusive household for your husband's? Or how a woman as strong as you, an immigrant in a new country, who raised four children, worked a full-time job on an overnight shift, put us all through school while earning your nursing degree, could accept a life of abuse. You not only accepted it; you were an active participant in it, so completely and utterly co-dependent that it seemed you didn't have a mind of your own. Yet worst of all, you passed this abuse on to your children, the people you were sworn as a mother to protect.

Let's go back almost to the beginning: I'm eleven and just starting junior high school. It's the morning after the night you'd taken a particularly bad beating from your husband, one that not even the police could stop since you wouldn't let them in, and then you yelled at us kids for calling them in the first place. I cornered you in the kitchen and asked, "Mama, why do you stay?"

You looked at me, face bruised, spirit broken and answered, "Because of you."

With those words, my heart wedged itself in my throat and stayed there for eighteen years.

"Because of *me?*"

"Yes, because of you. I want all you kids to finish college before I leave."

"It's because of me that you allow yourself to be beaten, shamed and humiliated? Because I'm the last child to go to college, and until I leave, you'll stay?"

"Yes."

Four years later I started college at fifteen. I'd finished junior high school in two years and high school in two years.

But you stayed.

Four years later, I graduated college.

But you stayed.

Ten years later, you were still there.

Although I carried the burden of guilt for your pain, the burden that you gave me, it was never about me; it was always about you. I know this now. I wish I'd known it then.

I don't believe in marriage, I don't believe in fidelity, I don't believe in love...and I blame you. A home without love is useless; all it does is perpetuate abuse. A home without love is like a room without walls, a bed without a floor. Pointless. Why would two people stay together for almost fifty years, yet not like each other very much? How could two people build a family without knowing what the word really means? How could your husband, my father, have three different families yet threaten to kill *you* if you leave him? Why did you put up with it? Why did you make your children put up with it? Why did you turn around and take it out on us? I've searched my whole life for the answer to these questions, yet I know I'll never find them.

As the years passed, I watched my siblings' relationships play out almost exactly as yours did, with infidelity, emotional abuse, co-dependency, and regret. My lack of emotional commitment is part and parcel of your dysfunctional co-dependent relationship. If you don't commit, you don't get hurt, I thought. Oh, how I wish it were true.

I wrote you a letter when I was in my twenties outlining all the reasons why you were a bad mother and why I hated you. Then I mailed it and didn't speak to you for two years. On your deathbed you gave it back to me, though the pages were creased and worn, and the type faint, it was still in its original envelope. In one of your few moments of clarity, you told me that you weren't angry; in fact you weren't even surprised. Instead, you said that it was so like me to speak my mind. That's what made me so much stronger than you. And it's one of the things you loved the most about me. You knew I would never end up like you. And for that you were proud of me.

You were right. When I was still very little, I promised myself I'd never end up in an abusive relationship, that I'd never end up in a loveless marriage, and that I'd never accept infidelity, that I'd rather be alone. But as I've grown up and gone through my own relationships, I've come to understand you a little better, not completely, because you never fully understood yourself. But little by little, I've come to see the inherent compromise in relationships, especially when children are involved, especially when you are in love.

I understand a little better now how you, a woman with barely a junior high school education, who'd been with the same man since she was thirteen, could think she had so few options. I've come to understand how you could feel adrift and alone in a new country. I've come to understand the particular emphasis your generation placed on "till death do us part." But as long as I live, I'll never understand how you championed me yet never championed yourself. You loved every word I've ever written, and shamelessly plugged my books and me to anyone who would listen and to quite a few who tried not to.

I know that more than anyone else, you'd understand my need to write you this new letter, because you understood, better than most, my need to write. I inherited that from you. You know that I don't write to be *understood*; I write in order to *understand*. I write to make sense of it all, to learn about myself and about where I come from, if only so I can understand where I am going and how I can get there.

I'd always wondered how I could be your daughter yet be so different from you. But as I sit here writing this, I see now that we're not so different. I look around and see oddly enough, that my place, though light-years from our old house, is not so much unlike it. I have Papa's love of plants and antique rugs, and I have your eye for pictures, which we both frame and arrange in hanging collages.

This realization sent me to a family photo album and I was rocked when I saw, in a new light, the photos of the house I grew up in. The living room was almost the exact same light blue of my bedroom, and the kitchen the same bright yellow as my kitchen and bathroom. And so it goes. The further you go away from your origins, the closer you get to finding yourself right back where you started. And you know what, it's not such a bad place because I now know where I got my style, my drive and my strength.

So I forgive you, Mama, for all the anger and hurt I've been carrying around. I have to. I won't take it to my grave or let it send me there early, like it did you. For everything else, I thank you. I have to, because without you, I would not be who I am today.

All these things I have to say to you, but as I stand there holding you in my hands, the words just won't come.

Carol Taylor is the author of seven books, among them Brown Sugar, *the bestselling four-book erotic series. Her novel,* The Ex Chronicles, *was published in 2010. The follow-up novel,* The Ex Chronicles: Plan B, *was published in spring 2013 in a four-book novella series titled* Insignificant Others, *with a new installment published every six months. A former Random House book editor, she has been in publishing for over eighteen years. Find her books and her work at BrownSugarBooks.com, or insignificantothersbooks. blogspot.com or follow her on twitter.com/iobooks*

Battling Love
Dominique Jackson

Dear Mah,

Remember that day when I tried to save your life? I was fourteen, scrawny, and armed with the strength that knowing someone you loved was going to die unless you did something gives you.

I grabbed his cane.

And you were broken. Face schism-ed; blood trickling from the cracks and he had your neck in his hand and was ready to slam his combat boot into its pulpy pieces again. Mah, I had to save you.

I jumped on the bed.

Did you know I already felt guilty because there was another fight, an apartment ago and I happened to be away—out roaming the neighborhood in the name of hanging with my posse of friends? I heard he tried to get your beat-up body onto a lit electric stove. I was not there to save you. But James was. And even though you survived unburned, I think I still cried for a week. I certainly gave up hanging with my friends. I also gave up being away too long. I became a homebody.

And it paid off. For this fight I was there at the very beginning. Before punches were thrown, I watched and became an instant referee. That was my role. Standing back and calling the fouls; yelling out plays that the participants in this match would ignore.

"Stop!"

"Don't say that!"

"Leave her alone!"

I couldn't run into the ring and take my place right beside you, Mah. Even though nature made him powerful and left us out-matched, I could not run into the fight, fist whirling, right away. It's disrespectful for a girl to hit her father even if he hit her mother first.

Mah, all I had was my voice. So I'd scream words that became mantras. Words that I later realized seeped too deep into my spirit.

"I hate you!"

"I hate my life!"

And then in my final acts of desperation, right before my hoarse voice would give out completely, in a tattered-shriek, I'd beg my father to answer this one question: "Why don't you love me?" Because certainly if he loved me, he'd stop hitting you—for me.

So there we were again, in another battle that this time started because my father wanted to sell the microwave oven and you were long tired of losing things. So instead, you fought to keep it. You were thirty-two, a mother of four girls and married to a drug-addicted man.

It was only when the tides changed that I'd jump in, only when the slaps and punches turned too brutal to just stand there and yell. This time it was when he traded his fist in for the steel-toed work boot and you hung limp, no longer trying to punch back, that I knew I had to choose between disrespect and salvation.

On the bed I held the cane horizontally in both hands. From behind, I placed it under his chin—against his Adam's apple. Using his back as leverage, I pulled with more heart than might and I held on, and I didn't let go, and I don't know if I held my breath, or if my head was thrown back, mouth opened and roaring at the ceilinged-sky. But I do know I held on until he let go.

Mah, remember when you came home from the hospital? I was

still in warrior-battle mode. It was still you and me against him. He was in jail, but I felt the only way for us to stay protected, the only way for you to do for us what your physical power could not, was for you to take him down for once and for all. We had to press charges. Against your husband; against my father; against our abuser. With the used camera I got for Christmas, I took pictures of your precious, battered face.

Mah, you were taking your meals in through a straw! My six-year-old sister cried when she saw you because she thought you were a monster and not our mother. It was me who wiped your face, who gave you liquids, who stayed after my three sisters were taken to our grandmother's house while you recovered. And what did you do? You destroyed the film—the evidence that I thought we were going to use to press charges.

In those days after, you didn't talk to me. You didn't tell me the things that might have made a difference in my life. Like I was pretty. Yes, you could have sat me, the wide-eyed witness, down, stroked my hair and told me, of all things, I was pretty. Plain and simple. Because by that time I had made up in my mind that ugly things took beatings. We were both battered. I'd spend years trying to make up for this. Overachieving to hide the ugly. Overdoing because I live in a perpetual state of trying to prove I'm worthy. I tell myself I deserve love. I do.

When you came home from the hospital and he was still in jail, you should have sat me down on that same bed I hopped on and told me a thing or two about love such as:

"Love doesn't look like this."

"Love doesn't come with fear."

"You don't hurt what you love." Ever!

I was old enough, fourteen, and a veteran in this war, so yes, you should have explained all the reasons, each and every single one, of why you stayed when flight would have made us stronger. Or better yet, why you never fought hard enough to leave. At the very least, Mah, you should have told me why you destroyed the film—our last attempt at saying no man has the right to put his hands on us.

Instead I was left to my own little girl-almost-a-woman assumptions. One says love is a woman's greatest weakness and the only way to stay safe on this earth is to never fall in love. That's my battle, love—it feels like the biggest betrayal I know.

And it's true, Mah, as women we want nothing more than to be a helpmeet, a champion of the person we love most—our men. And we believe with all our hearts that our love is strong enough to pull him through anything—falls on hard times, being between jobs, if he occasionally loses his temper. We believe our love is life-changing, mood-altering, mind-blowing.

And we are nurturers naturally. So armed with love and our elixir of nurture, we will put that man we love before all things— even our children. Even our good ol' common sense. So when we discover he has a drug habit he can't shake and soon enough begins selling all that we own, we forget about caution and we call on our love to save him. And we are hopeful that a change can come and he will go back to being the man we first fell in love with; the father he used to be to our children. This is what you sold, Mah. This is the story you sold when what you should have done was let him walk out of our lives while taking that microwave with him.

You know, Mah, today, twenty-two years later, I can separate where I went wrong in my girlhood assumptions—love is not weak and in the right hands, it is the greatest power we have. But I also know I have another hurdle to jump. Sometimes I'm still that girl on that bed holding a cane to my father's neck. I have to let go. I have to learn how to let it go.

I once asked you a question. "Mah, give me ten reasons why you stayed." I shifted the phone in my ear. "Think about them, I'll call you back in an hour."

"I don't need an hour," you said. And I waited to hear this great explanation of an answer. You continued, "I stayed because I wanted my daughters to have a father." You paused. "My father had always been in my life and I thought one was supposed to be in yours, too." And that was it. But I couldn't let it be it—it wasn't poetic enough, so I tried to bounce a whole slew of reasons off on you. I wanted something colorful, perhaps dramatic. He did have that run-in with the mafia that time—maybe he terrorized you in to staying? I wanted one of those Oprah-inspired "aha" moments. He was the provider, you stayed at home with us; perhaps you couldn't afford to leave? I wanted you to pretend you had been to therapy and get all psychosomatic with me. Remember that tumor they had to remove from your brain? Maybe it stemmed from the boot incident? You laughed and just like that, rejected the ideas I tried to give you. I felt unsatisfied.

But Mah, you know what? I think I had the question all wrong. Why you stayed with a man you knew since grade school and started dating at sixteen is really irrelevant. It happens. But this right here, right now is what I believe I really want to know. Mother, what do you think about love?

I talk to my mother every day, but it hadn't always been like this. For years I had blamed the tragedy that had become our lives on her. Yes, it's true that she wasn't the one who turned into a mean, abusive person when she'd drink alcohol. And she certainly wasn't the one who made a good part of her living pulling robberies and breaking and entering. And no, she was not the one who discovered crack in the '80s and was in love with it by the '90s. But our lives—the multiple evictions, the food stamps, the nothingness of Christmases and the nonexistence of back-to-school clothes and even food was all her fault because to me she was very, very weak. Why? Because she chose to stay married to my father—a man who dismantled our lives for rocks and pipes.

My mother, high school diploma-less, who sometimes moonlighted as a beach motel maid, who could not afford a four-dollar African Pride relaxer for my hair right before I went off to the summer camp I'd charmed my way for a scholarship, was never my hero nor my friend. She was my enemy. She represented a group she, by example, taught me to despise—weak women.

I didn't respect her. I didn't respect myself. Two years after the fight that landed my mother in the hospital and my father in jail—where he remained off and on for sixteen years—I became pregnant. I was sixteen. I was an angry girl. And who took the brunt of my anger? My mother.

This is nothing to be proud of I admit; however, there were times when she and I would physically fight. The last and most epic was right before my senior prom—I used makeup to cover up the evidence. I was sixteen, a mother myself, and she was thirty-four, a woman who was desperately trying to hold her life together. A parent who was present and there for her children yet I assigned her the blame of my father's bad habits and my condition; I made sure she felt the full force of my resentment. How did we survive that?

I'm more compassionate now. Since becoming a woman, I have seen up close and personal the slippery slope that womanhood can be—such a tricky terrain to navigate.

So somewhere between then and now, I rediscovered my mother—a kind woman with quick wit and stories, even of the abuse she survived, which would have you laughing for days. My mother—is a joy to be around, life of a party, and a presence requested at all family gatherings. My mother—who works a job, comes home and cares for her grandkids, and has kept the same roof over her head for twenty years. She's come a long way. I am so proud of her.

My mother is not mean-spirited or bitter. She does not feel sorry for herself and does not hold on to the past. A woman who by the very definition lived a majority of her life victimized has never once (in any of my memories) carried herself as a victim. That's huge! But let's be clear, there is one thing she cannot stand—my father, and we laugh about it now. We do. How strong is that?

Today my mother is my best friend. I do a lot of things for her. And because she knows struggle, she made a way so I'd never have to struggle in the ways she did. In a selfless act, she changed the trajectory of my life by taking custody of my then sickly four-year-old son, who'd have ten to twenty seizures a day, every day and would at times spend days and weeks at a time hospitalized. My mother never once buckled and threw up her hands saying she couldn't do it. She was used to fighting, hence caring for a sick child so her daughter could have a future was easy. She didn't bat an eye. In 1997 I went off to become a soldier in the U.S. Army where I made it to the rank of E-6 in four years. Fast.

My mother is brave!

She once allowed me to keep a scraggly alley cat that I found in an abandoned field I'd play in. She also knows I write stories built from the events that's happened in our lives. She lets me. When I sit and reexamine our lives—her life in particular—she answers my questions even though she knows the details will end up in my books.

If I get my way the whole-wide world will know our stories. She doesn't mind. I think somewhere deep down inside she knows this is my therapy. And the most amazing thing is we can laugh about these stories, even until we cry—including the episode over the microwave.

"I've always fought for you," she'd tell me, "I even fought to keep the microwave. I said, 'Nah, you ain't taking this out the house. My girls need this. I don't cook, either.'" But for real, she said she'd rather seen that microwave broken on the floor than in the posses-sion of a drug dealer.

I talk to my mother every day because I understand her, and every fight she's been in, she sincerely feels it was for us—her daughters who managed to survive the ugliness of her trying to figure it out. The ugliness of her falling in love with a man who'd succumb to the '80s crack-cocaine epidemic. To this day, her daughters do not smoke nor do drugs and only drink very limitedly if at all. They hold down homes and jobs and never once suffered from the physical abuse of a man. They are awesome mothers and wives and for the most part, they survived their childhoods un-scathed. How wonderful is that?

As for me, who could be classified as one of her challenging daughters, today I hold an associate's degree in Database Tech-nology and a bachelor's in Computer Information Systems with an emphasis in programming languages. I graduated with both de-grees Summa Cum Laude. I work as a computer engineer, I live debt-free, own homes and a few businesses. I earn well into that elusive six-figure salary, single-handedly. I'm the mother of one child. I'm not married—although I haven't ruled it out, I'm still working through those love issues and fears. For the most part I'd say I'm doing okay. I'm doing better than okay. After all, I'm able to use my life as material for the books I write and the colorful stories I tell—a talent I got from my mother. I am a woman who comes from an abusive situation, a drug-addicted father, having a child at sixteen and being homeless and on my own by seventeen—so yes, just like my mother, I've come a long way and I'm very proud of that. I'm very proud of us—my mother and me.

When Dominique Jackson is not (badly) painting copies of Picassos, she writes. She is the author of a collection of poetry, All Black Girls Ain't Got Rhythm, *a collection of short stories grounded in Hip-Hop, and* Holler at the Moon, *her debut novel. She is currently working on a second novel,* Twice on Sundays. *She currently lives in Northern Virginia with her twenty-year-old son.*

What I Thank You For
Pat Tucker

When I think about writing a thank-you letter to my mother, I'm unsure of exactly where to begin. And that's actually a very good thing. You see, unlike many women, I am very fortunate in that I share a very close relationship with my mother. I say "many women" because over the years, I've met women who are stunned silent when they learn the extent of the closeness my mother and I share. But I'm not alone; I have a younger brother and a younger sister, and each of us share this unique closeness to my mother. She's simply lovable that way. And she loves unconditionally, with my faults and all.

My mother was born and raised in Belize, Central America. She was one of sixteen children in a country that's a step above a Third World country. She often told me that before she had children, she knew she wanted to give her children a better life than the one she had and each and every day, I can honestly thank her for staying true to that promise. You see, it was not an easy thing to do. My mother's mother owned acres and acres of land in Belize and all she wanted to do was leave a legacy for her two daughters. One of them gave birth to my mother and for that I'm eternally grateful. I come from a long line of strong, hard-working women.

Things were never easy for my mother, but she stepped up to each and every challenge. When I was five years old, my mother was terminally ill and hospitalized. Doctors thought her days were numbered for certain, but God had other plans. Members of her very own family had already written her off; my father, her husband at the time, left. I suppose thoughts of his wife's probable demise were too much for him to handle. But when he left, he took my brother and me with him, back to Belize, back to his homeland. My father was also born and raised in Belize. But he and my mother migrated to the United States after my grandmother met and married a United States citizen.

I don't know what went wrong in their marriage. I'm not sure why he decided leaving his wife in the hospital, then taking her small children was a good idea, but that's exactly what he did. He obviously didn't know nor understand the power of a strong black mother. Because when my mother recovered the very first thing she did was track us down. Back then, we didn't have access to technology and resources the way we do today. This battle was my mother's, and hers alone, and she met the challenge. Despite all she went through to bring us back to the United States and the struggles she endured to raise us as a single mother, what I'd like to thank her for is something else altogether.

My mother has always worked hard all her life. Her high school education meant she'd have to succeed with a blue-collar job, and there were many times when one simply wasn't enough, so she'd take another. She did whatever she had to in order to provide and made sure we had everything we needed. What I'd like to thank my mother for most is her dogged determination. She knew firsthand how hard life was as an immigrant with limited education and resources, and she didn't want that for her children. Life wasn't easy, but she did the best with what she had. As a child I didn't understand the true struggle my mother had to endure just to keep food on the table and a roof over our heads.

I developed a very strong personality early in life. That strong personality was always coupled with a lot of sass. When old people used to say, watch your mouth, in more cases than not, they were probably talking to or about me. I can vividly remember my mother's frustration with me over the fact that I could not stop talking. I talked in church, I talked in school, and I talked back to adults when I thought I could get away with it. But what probably bothered my mother the most was the constant complaints from teachers and educators about my constant chatter. No matter how much I tried, I couldn't stop talking. If this happened today, I'm sure I would've been labeled as a kid with attention deficit disorder. Back then, the adults had little tolerance for me and my affliction. It was especially bad in school.

My mother would helplessly explain to me that if my mouth was open while the teacher was talking, there was no possible way that I could've been listening, and learning. She was frustrated and at her wits' end when she finally decided she simply couldn't take it anymore.

Aggravated, discouraged, and at a loss about what to do next, she decided to punish me in a way that she thought was her very last hope. One day after being sent home from school for talking back to the teacher who had had enough, my mother didn't even yell or scream.

"I'm tired," she said.

I rode in the car quietly because I knew I was in trouble and I had no idea what she had up her sleeve. The sad thing was after I'd get into trouble, I really felt bad. The last thing a single mother with three kids could afford to do was pick up her wayward child from school in the middle of a workday.

"I don't know what else to do to make you understand, you can't shoot off at the mouth and talk to teachers any kind of way," she said.

In my head, I thought about all kinds of things I could say. I wouldn't dare utter the words aloud, but because I talked so much, I had a reply for every complaint she threw out. Once I realized I was in trouble, I knew I needed to keep my mouth shut. On this particular day, when we arrived home, my mother was still very quiet. It was eerie to me how calm she was when she moved around the house. I knew she was upset and having her scream or shout out would've been better than the silent treatment.

"You just won't listen, and I'm tired," she said.

But this time as she spoke, she walked toward my bedroom. Her quietness had already put the fear of Jesus in me, because the unknown was always the worst. I watched as my mother removed the small record player from my room and all of the records that I loved to listen to. When she was finished, she removed the little black and white TV that I enjoyed watching. These were the things that helped me pass time and enjoy being a kid. By the time she was finished, my room had been stripped of any and everything that might bring me joy through entertainment.

"You are to stay in this room. You've got plenty of books, pens, pencils, and notepads," she said. "And for the next two weeks, that's all you can have. When you come home from school, do your homework, eat your dinner, take your bath and come into this room and close the door."

I watched as she explained the new rules to me. I had been on restriction many times. Restriction was like mini-jail for delinquent kids. One year I had just gotten off of a thirty-day restriction when, on my birthday, I got right back on again! So punishment was nothing new or foreign to me. But her new trick was something different.

At first, I had to write lines. I had to write that "I will not talk while the teacher is talking," and I had to write them at least one thousand times. By the time it was over, I was so sick of that phrase.

Spending time alone in my room forced me to reflect on my behavior. I had no idea why the things I had to say seemed so much more important than what our teachers had to say, but that's how it was for me. I didn't understand then the importance of doing what was expected at school or anywhere else. I always had something to say. Out of sheer boredom and frustration, I picked up one of those many books, and the rest was history.

Hey, Mommy,

An old but wise cliché warns that we should give flowers while our loved ones are still around to appreciate them. With that in mind, I try to shower you with praise as frequently as possible. You always knew what was best for me often, before I understood it myself. Your patience and dogged determination laid a foundation for the woman I would become.

Because you didn't give up, even when I had frustrated you to the point of no return, your hard work has paid off in a big way. I am an educated, successful woman who handles challenges with poise. Very few words could capture the emotions that fill my heart when I think of all you've done for me. As a child, I had no way of knowing what you were up to or how this would turn out. But one of the most profound things you did was instill the love for the written word in me. You see, that form of punishment, that you had to resort to too many times to count, has had a profound and lasting impact on my entire life.

Years ago, as I sat inside that room surrounded only by books and notepads, I was freed. I was exposed to so much through those stories. From the comfort and safety of the bedroom you provided,

I was able to travel to foreign places, meet new and interesting characters, and look at things from a completely different perspective.

When I thought I had run out of options in that empty room, I opened a book and realized the options were endless. You equipped me with an insatiable thirst for the written word that would carry me through my adult life.

With just the right amount of coaxing from you, I developed a strong passion for both reading and writing. That passion is what laid a solid foundation for my career as a journalist and as a nationally published author. Again, we may never know if it was your plan all along, but I think it paid off for us both. It really doesn't matter if you knew what you were doing at the time.

To this day, when we discuss my storylines, plots, and characters, I'm never lost on the fact that it was all because of you. It was you who helped set the groundwork for a lifelong gift that has enabled me to touch the lives of so many others. So when I say I thank you, it comes from the deepest depths of my very soul.

Regardless, it's now my turn to pay it forward. I don't expect the same elaborate results because I know it's not easy to re-create perfection. But I figure it won't hurt and I certainly can't go wrong when offering my children the same gift you gave to me. I started while they were in the womb. I read to them nightly, and now encourage them to read to each other. Each of my two children enjoys reading and understands the importance of reading and writing.

So while I could thank you for the very life you've given me, or my strong sense of self, it's the one small thing that has done so much for me. Who would've thought the girl who couldn't stop spewing words at the mouth, would one day get paid to share her words, and that's exactly what I continue to do.

There are so many times when thank you doesn't even seem to be enough. I am so lucky to have a mother like you. Just as I did when I was a child, I continue to learn valuable lessons that I hope will one day be passed along to my own daughter.

Lovingly,

Patty

Pat's work has been featured on the "Tom Joyner Morning Show," Essence.com, Yahoo Shine, Ebony *magazine, and a slew of TV and radio stations. By day, Pat Tucker works as a radio news director in Houston. By night, she's a talented writer with a knack for telling page-turning stories. A former television news reporter, she draws on her background to craft stories. Pat has worked for ABC, NBC, and Fox TV and radio stations. Pat's novel* Football Widows *is headed for the big screen as it's been optioned for a movie.*

Naomi to Your Ruth

Victoria Christopher Murray

Dear Nana:

The thirty-five years that I have known you have made you much more than my mother-in-law. You are truly my mother.

I didn't always know this. I didn't know that a mother-in-law and a daughter-in-law could share the kind of relationship that you've fostered between us. When your son, Ray, and I met in New York, I never had to think about his family. Everyone he loved lived three thousand miles away and for such a long time, I felt like it was Ray and me, just the two of us together. That time in New York gave Ray and me a chance to really become close, to develop a loving relationship.

But of course, once we became engaged, I had to meet you. Honestly, I tried to figure out a way to get out of that first meeting when we flew to Los Angeles for a short vacation. I thought about faking the flu, or pretending that I'd broken my ankle. "Maybe," I told Ray, "we can say that I had some kind of family emergency in New York and I had to catch the first thing smokin' back to the East Coast." I needed something, anything, not to have to meet my about-to-be mother-in-law.

Of course, Ray just laughed and said that you were going to love me as much as he loved me. Of course, I knew he was lying.

How could you love me? You were going to be my mother-in-law and just that word put fear in me. I had visions of a woman who would be able to rival the fable of the evil stepmother or even the Wicked Witch of the West. (After all, you did live in Los Angeles.) In my mind, I could actually see you on your broom, hovering low over the airport, waiting for me to have the audacity to land in your town.

But then, Ray and I arrived in L.A. and drove to your home in Gardena. And I will never forget the way you opened the door, the way you looked me up and down, the way you smiled, the way you said, "You must be Victoria."

I didn't even have a chance to respond before you swept me into your arms and held me as if you'd always known me, as if you loved me already, as if you always would. Then, you stepped back and said, "My middle name is Victoria, so we're already connected."

Nana, you have no idea how much your words meant to me that day. With your words and your actions, you erased every negative thought, feeling, belief I had about mothers-in-law. For the rest of the afternoon, I sat in that beautiful backyard and wondered about the tales of the evil in-laws.

Over the years, I could not believe how our relationship had grown. Your door was always open to me. I could talk to you about work, I could talk to you about family, I could talk to you about your son. And we'd lie on your bed and just talk; your heart was always open.

But it wasn't the love that you showed me at our first meeting, nor the love that was fostered over the years that meant the most to me. The greatest love I received from you came in the middle of our tragedy. Our broken hearts connected over the loss of the man that we both loved in very different ways.

From the moment I called you, Nana, to tell you that devastating news, you wrapped your love around me and never let me go. You were by my side for all of my sorrow, holding me physically and emotionally and spiritually. You were my strength.

But then weeks later, we sat together and had that conversation that changed my life. You asked me if I wondered why you never cried.

I told you that I never wondered, but the truth is, that I did. Not about you crying. I figured that you were being Nana, the strong woman whose faith had carried her through so much. I'd never seen you shed a tear before; I didn't expect to see you cry now. But I did wonder what it was like for a mother to lose her child? I did wonder how you were handling that.

And you explained it all to me.

"I haven't cried because I've cried so much for my children. All of their lives I've cried and I've prayed. And, maybe I just don't have any tears left." Then, you said, "But there was no reason for me to cry for Ray. When I saw him in that casket, when I saw how peaceful he looked, I knew he was where he was supposed to be. No matter the circumstances, he was finished."

Do you remember that I was already crying when you took my hands into yours and you added, "But you're where you're supposed to be, too, Victoria. You're here. You're not finished. And, I'm going to make sure that you accomplish everything that God has for you here."

I sobbed so hard then. Not because your words made me sad, but because you made me glad. That was the first time I realized that I could have a future without Ray, and I wouldn't be doing it alone.

To me, that was the day when you were no longer my mother-in-law. To me that was the day when I truly became your daughter. To me, that was the day when you became my Naomi and I, your Ruth.

There is no doubt that I knew my mother and father would always be there for me with anything I needed, especially with their love.

But there is something about the love I share with you. We are the only two people on earth who loved Ray at the deepest level. And even though the bond that brought us together is gone, my love for you is stronger than it's ever been.

A decade has passed since we lost Ray, but that has nothing to do with our relationship. Ray is not the reason for us anymore. We exist because you and I were meant to be.

Over the past years, I've wondered if I was created by God to be Ray's wife or to have you as my second mother. I'm not sure... both roles have been great blessings in my life.

As we've talked about many times, I know that one day I will remarry and that time is probably coming soon. But one thing I know is that while I may have a new husband and he may have a mother, she will never be able to take your place. After all, she will be a mother-in-law...and you are already my mother.

Nana, you just need to know that I honor you, cherish you and love you. And, no matter what the future holds for either of us, I will love you always and in all ways.

Victoria

Victoria Christopher Murray is a graduate of Hampton University and received her MBA from New York University. She self-published her first novel, Temptation, *before Time Warner rereleased it. Since then, Victoria has written more than twenty-plus novels. Victoria's latest novel,* Never Say Never, *is a 9/11-inspired story that* USA Today *lists as a book club recommendation.*

The Epitome of a Woman
ReShonda Tate Billingsley

As a little girl,
I used to admire those fancy women on TV,
Their cars, their jewelry, their lives,
like them I wanted to be.
As I grew a little older,
my goals they started to change.
I wanted to conquer the world
become a household name.
I looked up to Oprah Winfrey and Maya Angelou,
Alice Walker and Mae Jemison,
just to name a few.
These were hardworking sistas,
and like them I wanted to be.
I wanted to follow in their footsteps.
They emulated womanhood to me.
And while I was doing all this dreaming,
making these big plans for my life,
I paid little attention
to the woman who chose to sacrifice.
I didn't notice her working two jobs
just to make ends meet.
After all, she wasn't rich or famous;
she took a back seat.

It didn't matter to me then that she sometimes went without,
So I could have a better life and
that there'd be no doubt,
That she loved and would provide for me
until her dying day.
She'd love me unconditionally and
support me along the way.
My childhood dreams are gone,
the truth can now be known.
For the epitome of a woman
I can look inside my home.
I take nothing away
from the successful sisters of the past.

But I now know that my mother ranks in their same class.
She doesn't have their success,
their fame or their fortune.
But she does possess something that to me is just as important.
She had the faith and the strength
to make a way when there was none.
Through the tears and the sweat, her work was never done.
It took me a while to see that I need not look to any other,
For if I want to see the epitome of a woman,
I can just look at my mother.

I have one of those mother-daughter relationships where we share everything. Even things I didn't share when I was younger (because my mama was crazy), I openly shared as an adult when we crossed the line of "I'm not your friend, I'm your mama." My mom is now among my best friends. She knows the good, the bad and the ugly of my life. So I thought writing this letter to her would prove challenging. What would I say that I hadn't already said before? There was nothing to say. Until she wasn't there for me to say it.

On August 17, 2012, I had a book release party to celebrate my newest release. As she usually does, my mom came out to support me. Toward the end, she came over to kiss me goodbye and headed out. About fifteen minutes later, a woman came racing in the party looking for me. We raced outside and my mom was sitting in a vehicle, bloodied. Turns out she had passed out in the parking lot and a passer-by had seen her lying there. Thank God she had on white pants because it was pitch black and the parking lot had no lights. The woman stopped and helped my mom up. My mom, dazed and confused, said she had just tripped. At that moment a lady was leaving the local drugstore nearby. She looked at my mother's eyes and suggested that we get her to the emergency room right away, which we did despite my mom's protests. It was there that doctors told us that my mom had a brain tumor that had apparently been growing ten years. Long story short, we went into surgery and my mother had a stroke on the table. She is recovering, slowly but surely. It has been one of the most difficult journeys I have ever had to take.

This is my letter to my mother.

Dear Mom,

Today was the first day in seven months that you got to come home, or rather to *my* home. We still haven't taken you to yours. After six hospitals, three surgeries, and countless tears, we think taking you home will be too devastating because you can't stay.

Right now, I'm not sure how much you can process. Each day brings a new awareness, each day you can do a little bit more than you could the day before. But you are still just a shell of your former self.

But still I rejoice.

Right now, I'm watching as you go through my jewelry box. You're trying on bracelets and rings and I smile. I smile because it used to drive me crazy when you got all in my stuff (I guess it was payback for my teen years.) I constantly fussed because you would take my stuff to wear before I even took the price tag off.

But now, it's a beautiful sight.

Just a month prior, your brain wouldn't even recognize that side of your body. The doctors said your brain wouldn't register that there was a hand, leg, anything on your right side. Now, you're trying to adorn your arm with Tiffany bracelets.

You still can't talk. Or walk. But through your tears, I see your determination. Through your frustration, I see your perseverance. You have taught me to appreciate the little things in life, the things we take for granted. The things we can never get back.

As I was preparing for my latest book tour, I made my to-do list. It was nearly a page long. Then, I thought about you and the lessons that I'd learned from you over the years. You always chided me about taking time for the things that truly matter in life. I thought about your words, tossed my to-do list, and came and spent the day with you.

We no longer can communicate verbally (although I'm confident that will one day change), but we now have what I call a love language. I'm learning to read you more, to feed off your nonverbal communication, to be in tune with your needs and wants. (Of course, it's not hard to decipher that eye roll you still give me.) Most importantly, I'm learning to appreciate the little things.

During the course of your recovery, I admit that my faith sometimes wavered. Thankfully, my friends (even those I'd never met on social media) prayed for me when I couldn't find the strength to pray for myself. And they prayed for you. We all did. You've always told me that prayer works. You were right. You've come a long way, and yes, you still have a ways to go. But in the midst of your struggles, if I know nothing else, I know God's got this. And my mother will emerge—bigger, better and stronger than ever.

I look forward to the day when you can walk through my walk-in closet, complain about "how you didn't raise me to keep my closet this dirty," then proceed to take whatever you want to wear. Yes, not only do I look forward to those days, but I will hand you whatever you want with a smile. Thankful that I got the greatest gift of all—quality time with you.

ReShonda Tate Billingsley is the national bestselling author of twenty-six books, including the nonfiction books, Help, I've Turned into My Mother *and* The Motherhood Diaries. *More information about the Houston native can be found at www.reshondatatebillingsley.com.*

Thank You Letter
By Trisha R. Thomas

There aren't many days I remember about growing up before the age of eight or nine. I wanted childhood to be over as quickly as possible. Memories are a funny thing, decidedly chosen by our subconscious. For me, I see a few spots on a calendar signifying birthdays and holidays. Most of my memories are from pictures. Those photos in the yellowing album tell full stories, none I could possibly conjure up on my own. Four years old, Easter, wearing the most precious floral dress in teal and pink pastel colors, white stockings and white patent leather shoes to match. Christmas morning, unwrapping the box nearly the same size as me revealing the brown-skinned doll with long silken hair that walked, talked, in a fluffy pink dress. I think I loved that doll.

We have no idea what kind of person we are going to become. The future has no relevance. As children, our goals are cut and dry; wake up, go to school, do as you're told, try to make new friends, and make your mother proud. At least these were my goals, the ones I remember. My friends, those girls in the pictures, from elementary to high school, used to call me a mama's girl. I liked it. They didn't understand that it was just me and you against the world. That I was the one you depended on after you and Dad divorced. There was nothing wrong with being "Mama's baby." You and I were on the same page. I was your movie date for Saturday matinees and you were my best friend who listened to my reports of the day. And like a best friend, you knew when to stay close and when to put a little distance. Sometimes I was sure you were psychic.

Like the day I stood in the mirror with the bathroom door closed, you knocked, and asked the loaded question. "What're you doing in there?"

I answered, "Nothing."

You knocked again, knowing instinctually there was something afoot. Of course you were right. I'd been in there too long, scissors in hand, looking in the mirror. What you sensed behind that closed door was your baby going through some kind of turmoil. I'd been quiet and moody, not unlike all girls my age. Those days when nothing felt right. Boyfriend drama. Girlfriend drama. If I try to recall exactly what was bothering me, I only remember being weary. I have the pictures to prove it. Sullen, depleted, wishing to get it all over with, whatever "it" was at the time.

Sixteen and defeated already, I'd seen enough of the trajectory ahead. I wanted to cut it off at the pass. So like you, I wanted to be happy again. Your pictures now told a bold new story. The one where you came home after shedding your favorite wig after stopping in the salon. You walking into the house, free. Your curly new do was cut close, sassy, and full of shine. Those same adjectives would describe your new personality. Light as air. Forty and fabulous, hand on hip wearing spanking-new Calvin Klein jeans to show off the curves and tiny waist no one knew you had. It hit me right then and there that you may not want to be my best friend anymore. What next, a date or two? You were on a new level of life. Happy. Where would that leave me? And all the while, I wanted that, too. I wanted to shed the pain and worry or everything irrelevant and start fresh. So I did the only thing I thought would get me there.

Standing in that bathroom, I began my new path of freedom. Off with my signature Stacy Lattisaw hair, the thick mane I was known for. The mask I was hiding under was suddenly gone. After the major chopping, I came out smiling. You smiled with me, though you couldn't believe what I'd just done. After all, it was Grad Nite. The biggest, popular event of the year for seniors to descend on Disneyland from dusk to dawn. Off I went, out the door wearing my shaved head. Those pictures will forever say loud and proud, all that I'd learned from being your daughter. Never let anyone else define you. Stand up when you're down and make that decision, whatever it maybe, that will bring you peace of mind.

You loved me hell or high water, never once criticizing my decisions. You taught me to admire without envy, love without possessing, and honor without smothering. You taught me mother's love. Thank you.

Trisha

Trisha R. Thomas is the author of the highly acclaimed Nappily Series best known for her debut novel, Nappily Ever After *(Random House). The Nappily Series speaks to the impossible beauty standards set for young girls and how it affects their relationships and careers far into adulthood. She has written eight novels and continues to share her talent with a multitude of readers who can't get enough of her beloved character, Venus Johnston. She's been a guest analyst on CNN,* Paula Zahn, *and* Headline News *sitting on panels with many notable spokespersons on self-esteem and beauty issues. She's been a guest at various events and fundraisers including the Alpha Kappa Alpha Regional Meeting, The Delta Sigma Theta Farwest Regional Conference, and numerous empowerment seminars on the craft of writing. She currently lives in Riverside, California with her family.*

Disappointing You
Denise Nguyen

Dear Mom,

I'm thirty-six years old. This means you must no longer be thirty-six, which is the age I would name you, with your youthful strength, your friends blended together by hilarity, your rebellion…and your wisdom, and your kindness, and your resiliency.

And I am unmarried, without a child, and you are in a prolonged state of confusion, but I am only living in despair, that I have failed you. It's been a terrible past seven years, with your hints and your friends making comments—you want a grandchild. You want me to have a husband and have a baby before it's impossible.

But who are we kidding? Can I really marry myself to somebody? I have seen you with my father, the bane of my emotional health. You fought him to save my life when I was a baby girl. He threatened me every week—threw things at me, shouted, picked me up to throw me out, struck me. I saw him push you back during a fight over me. I saw you yelling at him to defend me from his crazed accusations. I was scared for seventeen years for myself and for you. Why would I ever be willing to marry anybody when I could live alone and be safe from suffocation, from controlling abuse, and from an eruptive temper?

Still, I grieve. I am lonely, and I can't see an end of the tunnel. Maybe for the fact that I have a father that ruined me for life—or that you can't have a grandchild because I am attracted only to noncommittal and immature guys who eventually wish I were thin and sexy like the girls they see at work. Men who do not value or cherish me. Who hurt my feelings and abandon me for selfish pursuits.

But they do not hit me.

I wish you had left Dad. I wish you had bundled up my cheap kid clothes into a plastic bag and driven us off in the middle of the night in that wide, green metal car. I wish you had had the guts to try. Just to get a job and put us in an apartment in a shitty area of town with a Styrofoam chest as a refrigerator and a mattress on the floor as a bed. I know it would have been equally awful, maybe, but I wish it anyway.

I wish that standing up for me didn't get coupled with talks about how he put a roof over our heads so I "should be understanding." Now I am attracted to roofs. I obsessively desire houses I would buy and I avoid men who have good jobs. I am scared of wealthy successful men who want families and who ask me out. I don't know how to get married. I only know how to worry about money and retirement and how I am going to get healthcare when I am old and alone, dying.

Well, I die every day. Because having to grow up in the care of someone who might best be described as a manic-depressive maniac with narcissistic personality disorder and maybe a touch of borderline personality disorder to boot is enough to make anyone feel trapped.

You've gone a little sideways, too. I see your recently increasing demonstrations of what could be ADD and your inability to listen to anyone for longer than fifteen seconds. You weren't always like that. I surmise you might have post-traumatic stress disorder, after living with him so long.

I am sorry for you, Mom. You're vivacious and personable, and you have true sympathy for your friends, but nobody outside our family truly understands the mental and emotional torture you've undergone. Your husband was a monster, and you couldn't always prevent him from harming your children. And you felt you could not leave him in order for your children to have a roof over their heads and food on the table. And you let him shout at you so that your children might be spared, but had to see us disintegrate anyway.

I keep telling you that you are the best mother in the world, and you are an incredible person, but I want to say it, yes, you should have made different choices. Because I am a mess—a woman without a safety line, a pleaser, an overactive socializer, with too many friends and not enough passion, a depressed and scared person who cries every month and wonders why she isn't adequate.

I wouldn't say that to you, though, because I would have to be awful to want to hurt your feelings. You've been through so much already, for far too long.

But why won't you ever just quit him? Just leave? We're grown, now, and we have jobs, and we can all support you. But you insist he did his job as a father so you have to stay and take care of him.

I remember one time you said to me that you had told your sister that if you were found dead, he did it.

That was an obscure memory. It was overshadowed by my intense desire to die myself, the only escape route I could bear to face. The best hiding place I could imagine.

One time, after another grievous event, you made me promise never to kill myself. Sometimes, that promise I made has forced me to think of other ways to get through a dark, dark day.

Now he says things about how much he sacrificed to be the father his own father was not, and I heave and sigh to bite my tongue. He is self-congratulatory, patching over great gaping chasms of inadequacy with self-praise. It's called spin, that bullshit that he halfway believes. And because you would always say sympathetic, pitying things about him, I would not throw reality back in his face to further wound him.

But I resent it when he asks for affirmation. When he expects agreement and embellishment to his self-pleasing announcements.

I remember when you and I watched *American Beauty* together. Allison Janney played the wife of Chris Cooper's abusive and murderous character. You shocked me during the screening, when she was introduced as Wes Benton's mother. She was nearly coma-tose, unblinking, lost in a world of her mind. I didn't comprehend her, and thought, what is that? And then I heard you.

All you did was utter a single sound of understanding. It was a sympathetic and depressed "oh." I heard you groan that small, sad sound, and I realized with utter clarity that you *knew* her character in a flash because she represented a piece of you. You never acted like her, but you felt like her. That has haunted me ever since. You're always loud and lively, but that catatonic character was like you. Somehow. I've never seen that side of you. You're such a feisty, humorous person. But I heard you relate to her. And it scares me.

Maybe I'm not the only one who fights against giving up on an ordinary day.

I went to therapy against your wishes. You were so threatened by my declaration of need; you made it so taboo. I told you I needed it and you argued with me. Years later, I ate cheap tacos and spent my money on a therapist who got to know me for one year. Near the end of it, she said, "In your case, mere survival is a triumph." I burst into tears to know I had been understood.

Last month you told me you prayed to God to ask Him why he had not seen fit to send me a husband and give me a child. I am long past asking why. I used to think I would be a good mother, and my friends and acquaintances so often tell me I would be one—that I am patient, and kind, and honest, and plainspoken, and funny, and understanding. But I am starting to believe that God has cut our line short; that I only know how to survive. That a healthy and patient husband would render me useless to a child, because the best thing I could do as a mother is insert myself between my child and a psychopath; that I never learned how to raise a healthy kid.

Still, I grieve—for my meaningless survival—for your meaningless motherhood to a daughter who won't give you a grandchild—for my father, who never got over his past—and for my brothers, who are afraid to become just like their father.

As much as everybody at church admires you, and the length of your marriage, I pity you, Mom. What I have been afraid would break you if I told you is: that I am alone in life because of your choice to stay married to my dad. That it isn't just his fault. That it is partly yours.

I used to stay around toxic boyfriends without the ability to quit those exploitative, nonreciprocal relationships. Finally I got some power and left, and left, and left again. Now I don't even start. I trust gay men and straight women and my life is full of love, but despite a carefully developed circle of wonderful friends, I am all by myself. I am sorry for you, when you feel sorry for me, because I suspect you blame yourself. I love you and yet, although I forgive both you and Dad, I am exhausted by the long and excruciating past.

I want you to know that I don't hate myself as I once did, but I am living without the same foundation others seem to have. I also want you to know that I have not lived in vain. I've given to the poor, and I have helped my friends tremendously. I have loved. And I have achieved very many amazing things. Please do not pity me anymore. Even though I am alone in life, I am not worthless. And even though I am unmarried without children, you are not worthless. You saved me, and my life, day in and day out, from hunger, and hatred, and violence. I always will love you, and I hope this truth is more important to you than the rest of the truth.

Your daughter,

Denise Nguyen

Denise Nguyen is a fiction writer in New York.

Let it Start with the Mothers

Heather Rae

Dear Mama,

One of my very earliest memories is of your boyfriend Michael taking me to pick you up from work late one night at a go-go dancing at a club in Pocatello, Idaho. I remember peeking through a door as he and I waited outside. I was holding his big hand and I thought he was going to be my dad for a while. Through the door was a smoky eye-line to you, dancing in a cage in a fringed-panty outfit. I was confused, but mesmerized. Somehow, it was okay to be in a cage because that it was where you went to "work." In my mind, that meant it must have been of value.

I remember as a child your long, thick black hair and almond-shaped eyes. And I remember an early black cat named Ishtar. You had a small shop in Pocatello for a spell called Incense and Peppermint and I used to help you at your shop. You sewed and crocheted your clothing and it was beautiful. So many things of those times were colorful and velvet and lacy with music playing all the time.

You did something incredibly important in my life, among many things; you got me on a horse. We lived in Bellingham, Washington in an old, big house and I went to that hippie school where we made cookies for cooking class and then just ate the dough 'cause we felt like it. We went on field trips with the teachers to pick "mushrooms" but then never saw the mushrooms again. After school I went to ride horses. That was one of the first times I knew I was home.

There were things you did in my life that were so magical. You brought me to the piano and I played during my most formative years. We moved thirty-six times from my birth to age sixteen when I left, and that piano managed to get towed along in the back of your '66 Chevy, along with my first pony, Midgie. I remember writing my first songs and practicing in the mornings. My routine was this: feed my horse and the dogs, stir my little brother and practice piano. You supported my endeavors in a way that allowed me to truly develop into someone who does things, who seeks out life and who listens for the songbird in the evening light.

Idaho was perfect. Beautiful mountains, powerful rivers, handsome seasons, gentle folks, more land than people and horses, elk, wolves, bear and mountain lions. I could not be more thankful for being raised in a way that builds character and strength. I'm not a lazy person and if I had to survive in the woods, I could. I also learned from you and Grandma how to cook, bake, sew, look after others, grow food and get around the world with kindness.

Most significantly I want to thank you for life—for those months you had me in your body and the years you grew me up to be the woman I am today. I also want to thank you for doing the very best you could with the circumstances we faced, those enduring cycles of poverty, alcoholism, violence, and general disenfranchisement.

There is so much I have learned from you about living a spiritual life and knowing my role in the larger world. There were also very difficult times between us. And from the dark days I know I grew strong, but I also suffered. I've prayed so many times that I not pass along to my daughter what you passed along to me, and Grandma passed along to you. Unlike that, I want her to know herself as dignified and beautiful.

What healing we need. I see the seed for a global transformation of women's relationships to one another. Women need to heal with one another. Mothers and daughters need to heal. Sisters need to heal. The world needs to heal.

Let it start with the mothers.

Heather Rae

Heather Rae is an American film producer, director, and actress of partly Cherokee descent. She produced Frozen River *(2008), which won the Grand Jury Prize at the Sundance Film Festival as well as two Academy Award nominations and was acquired by Sony Pictures Classics. She is married and has three children.*

Reflections of You
Donna Hill

Dear Ma,

I can't tell you how many times I started this letter and stopped (all in my head of course). I couldn't seem to get the words out of my head and onto the page. I didn't know where to begin—or where it would end. Being the proverbial writer I was searching for the perfect opening sentence; the line that grabs the audience and propels them along the path of my pithy prose. Then there was a moment of revelation, that epiphany that all of my characters have (or should). I wasn't writing to entertain or to enthrall my fans. I was writing a letter to my mom to tell her what is in my heart and on my mind. I was writing a letter to the one person who knows me best. I realized *that* is what scared me—talking to you "in public," revealing things about me, about you, about us.

So many of those things ran through my head. How much could I say, should I say without pulling back the covers on "family stuff"? There was no easy path, no clear starting point, but one idea continued to surface—resilience. Without your resilience, I don't know where Lisa, David or I would have been, who we would be. It took courage and determination to pack up three kids and leave the home that you helped to build. Did I ever tell you that I still dream of that house, that I re-create it in my novels? There is a mixture of good and bad memories, things that I heard and witnessed—things that shaped me. For years after we left Putnam Avenue, the sound of jingling keys made my stomach curl and the hair on my arms tingle. The scent of rose body oil still unsettles me in all the wrong ways. Do you remember? It was more than three decades ago, and it still has a hold on me, but you somehow moved on and rebuilt your life from the ground up.

Rebuilding wasn't easy, either. I remember the days and days of spaghetti in every combination imaginable; spaghetti with sauce, without sauce, with butter and even with tuna! But we managed. We didn't starve. We were happy. And when the time was right, we moved from that first two-bedroom apartment with four people to a three-bedroom duplex with a yard. You did that. It was the first time on your own since moving from your mother's house (Nana) into marriage. Surely you got your grit from Nana who raised seven children virtually single-handed through the Depression and beyond. I know it must have been scary for you—and you did some scary things (but it will stay between us). But you never let on. You never said, "I can't do this," no matter how you may have felt. That single trait stuck with me. I don't know if it's good or bad, but I have it, too; the ability to keep up the façade of strength and resilience even when the world is crumbling around me.

Things did crumble from time to time, but you always, always managed to bounce back. That's why I knew when we all rushed to the hospital because the doctors had called "the code,' and were trying to save you—I knew that your resilience, your strength would win out. I knew that even though the doctors said you were down without oxygen—I knew none of that mattered.

Now nearly two years later, months of rehab, nurses, new meds, endless doctor visits, thankfully we can talk still about your beloved grandkids, my crazy work hours, the latest episode of *Downtown Abbey* and of course, *Scandal*, remind each other to get enough rest, promise to talk the next day—and we do.

And even though you are still hampered by a myriad of illnesses that make me weak thinking of them, you continue to persevere. You make sure your hair is done and your nails are done and your eyebrows are on. You're a "woman of certain age," that has earned you the right to say whatever is on your mind and you do! Like never forgetting to tell me how much you love me each and every time that we talk, even when I can hear in your voice that it is hard for you to breathe, or remind me to kiss the kids for you, or that you plan to put a few dollars in the mail for them (just like Nana).

It's all that stuff, Ma, and all the stuff that's just between us. The stuff that made you strong that you passed along to me. The stuff that we don't talk about, but we know it in our hearts.

I want to be able to keep telling you "stuff" and being reminded that you love me and to see you put on your eyebrows and tell me to kiss the kids. I know it's not possible forever, for long—but because I am you, because of you, I have the resilience and the courage to be *you* for my kids and hope that like you, I will have countless days to tell them that I love them, to share "stuff" said and unsaid, to create a place, if not in their lives, at least in their hearts that they will carry with them wherever they go.

Most of all I want you to know that these paltry words will never come close to express all the "stuff" between us. Me and you. I could not have done it without you. None of it. I thank you, Ma, for all that you did, do, endured, endure and sacrificed for me, for all of us; how you remain graceful and funny and irreverent and courageous and always resilient.

I love you more,

D

Donna Hill is an award-winning author with more than seventy titles in print. Three of her novels were adapted for television. She is an Adjunct Professor at Essex County College, Medgar Evers College and the College of New Rochelle.

She is an online Teaching Assistant for Ashford University and maintains a full-time job at the Office of the Brooklyn Borough President as a Writer. She holds an MFA in Creative Writing from Goddard College. She is the mother of three amazing young adults, and grandmother of four. Donna lives and breathes the written word and does so from the home that she shares with her family in Brooklyn, NY.

No Mama Drama

Danita Carter

First of all let me start by saying my mother and I don't have "Mother/Daughter Issues" that plague some people. Well, okay, there was that one time when I was sixteen and I ran away to my sister's house. I'm getting ahead of the story. How about I start at the beginning?

I'm from a tight-knit family. Growing up, I thought everyone had a mother, father, sister, brother, dog and lived in a house. Everyone on our block had the same family dynamics as mine, so my view was skewed. Our block was idyllic, racially diverse, hard-working, and had friendly neighbors who were like family.

My parents married young, and were married fifty-two years before my dad passed away. My mother was a stay-at-home mom for the first six years of my life. Most girls are "Daddy's Girls," but I can honestly say, I was both. As a baby, I'm told that I couldn't stand my dad, would cry when he picked me up, and would cry nonstop when my mom left the house to run errands. I'm told that I would sit on the floor by the door until she came back.

By the time I could walk, my mother and I would take the bus downtown (she couldn't drive at the time), and browse around until it was time for my sister and brother to come home from school. Being the youngest, I had my mother all to myself when they were in school and I loved it. When I started kindergarten, I can remember telling my mom, "Now, you don't go anywhere, until I get home from school."

She would smile, and answer, "I won't."

Growing up, my mother was the disciplinarian, which is ironic. You see my mother stands all of four-feet, ten-inches. Although she was small, she didn't take no mess. My mother was so youthful-looking, that at first the neighbors thought my father had three daughters. I can remember hot summer days, my mother outside playing Double Dutch with my sister and me. She was a lot of fun, but didn't cross the line. Mom would say in a heartbeat, "Don't think I'm one of your *little* friends. We're having fun, but I'm still Momma."

And we couldn't even think about clowning around in church! She would make her already tight eyes, even tighter, and give you the "Look." If I didn't stop fidgeting or whatever I was doing, she'd make her already small lips, even smaller, until they were just a slit. Oh, man, when I saw the tight-eyed-tight-lipped-look, I knew for sure I was in trouble. And I never wanted to hear her whisper, "Wait until we get home." Terror would descend upon me and I'd straighten up, stop squirming and pay attention to the sermon.

Growing up, I can remember sitting on my parents' bed, watching my mom getting ready to go out. She and my dad were members of various social organizations, and would dress to the nines—tuxedo, gowns, gloves, and plenty of glitz. My mom was the epitome of a lady—soft-spoken, well-mannered, and appropriately dressed for any occasion—I would say to her, "I can't wait to grow up, so I can wear lipstick, stockings and high-heels."

Mom would tell me, "Enjoy your childhood. You'll be grown soon enough." And she was right!

Being the youngest, at one point, I was the only child living in the house once my brother and sister moved out. My mother would take me downtown to see Buckingham Fountain (a popular tourist attraction in Chicago). We would have lunch, walk around all day and wait until the lights came on around the fountain. Seeing the lights change colors was like magic. My mother and I still talk about those times. I was her little running buddy (I still am)!

When my mother learned to drive, I loved going places with her. It would baffle me how she found her way around the city. It all looked so confusing to me with cars going in difference directions. I'd say, "Momma, how do you know where you're going?"

She would reply, "I read the signs." Her saying this was a revelation. It never occurred to me that the street signs provided vital information.

My parents loved them some Sears, Roebuck and Company (that's what it was called back in the day) and I loved going with them. At that time, Sears had a vast toy department, which was on the way to the automotive department. I would slow my gait as we passed the Barbies (I was a Barbie freak…still am.) I would give my mother that sad, doe-eyed look and ask if I could choose a friend for my other Barbies. My dad would say, "You have enough dolls."

My mom would chime in with, "Bill, she's only young once." And then she'd buy me another doll.

My mother made growing up a joy! I can honestly say without reservation that I had a FANTASITC childhood! Mom, I can never thank you enough for all you have done in my life. The following letter is a token of my appreciation.

Dear Mom (Momma),

On the eve of your eightieth birthday (I must say you're the youngest eighty-year-old I've ever seen, still wearing high-heels and playing cards until the wee hours of the morning), I'd like to say thanks for being the perfect role model. You taught me through example how to be a lady. You didn't allow me to walk around outside with curlers in my hair, or wear short-shorts, and totally forbade me from walking on the back of my sneakers.

Thank you, Mom, for teaching me self-respect. When braiding boys' hair was popular in high school, I called myself a master braider. Remember the day I was braiding my friend's hair and you had a fit? You called me in the house and told me that you didn't want to see me braiding hair ever again. At the time I couldn't understand what the big deal was. Years later, as an adult, I was driving down the street and saw a young boy sitting between a girl's legs and the sight had an inappropriate sexual connotation. Suddenly it struck me why you didn't want a boy sitting between my wide-open legs. As you said back then, "It just doesn't look nice."

Mom, you taught me the value of punctuality. You detested tardiness (and still do). I was never late for school, thanks to you. This important value transferred over into my adult life. Being on time for work and appointments, both professional and personal, is immensely important, and I thank you for instilling this in me.

During the holidays, you would come home after working all night, and start Thanksgiving dinner. You'd put the turkey on, make dressing, macaroni and cheese, greens, string beans, potato salad, bake pies and have dinner completely done by the time we woke up. So, I say thank you, Mom, for teaching me the importance of holiday traditions. Now we cook for you on the holidays, but you can still throw down.

It's time for the runaway story…I was sixteen and, as they say, "Feeling myself." I don't even know what the argument was about, but we had words. This was the first time I ever bristled up while talking to you, and you wasted no time letting me know that you were the woman of the house. I got my feelings hurt, and decided to get you back by running away to Denise's house. I stayed there for two days. To be honest, I wanted to come home the next day, but I was too embarrassed to say I was wrong for talking back to you. Dad came and picked me up, and you welcomed me back with open arms. I apologized and felt really stupid. Thank you for not holding my adolescent ways against me.

Mom, thanks for always believing in me! Whatever I wanted to do in life, you always told me that I could accomplish anything I put my mind to, and the way you said this, I knew it was true. I've had so many careers in my lifetime, from designing jewelry, and hats, to working on Wall Street, and now writing novels. You've been my main supporter every step of the way. You were so cute when you told all your church friends about my novels, and said I should come to the church and talk about my books. I replied, "Uhh…Mom, these books aren't for church." This was when I wrote my first steamy novel. Thanks for your constant encouragement; you're always telling me that one day my books are going to be made into movies and I believe you.

Everyone who knows me, knows I'm a fashionista. I loves me some clothes and this is thanks to you. I can remember coming home from school, going upstairs to my room, and discovering a new outfit, complete with tights and new ribbons, laid out on my bed. I would be so surprised. You taught me to respect my clothes and not throw them on the floor. You also taught me to change my school clothes the moment I came home, and put on my house clothes. To this day, I still change clothes when I come home. You also taught me to pick my clothes out the night before, so that I wouldn't have to rush in the morning. This is something I also do to this day. Thank you, Mom, for great organizational skills and fashion sense.

I am a neat freak! This is due in part to you teaching me how to clean the house thoroughly. During spring break while the other kids on the block were out playing, we were in the house cleaning up. You said, it was called "Clean Up Week" for a reason. Thank you, Mom, for teaching me to clean without taking shortcuts. I used to try to take short cuts, but you, being Johnny-on-the-spot, would call me out every time and say, "If you do it right the first time, you won't have to do it over."

Mom, thank you for your wisdom. There have been times when I didn't know which direction to take in life, and your wise words were so on time. After talking to you, I always feel so much better.

Thank you, Mom, for my spiritual upbringing. You taught me to read the Bible and believe in God. Whenever I get down, you refer me to a passage, and I must admit that after reading the word of God, I feel so much better. Your faith is unwavering and you've passed that on to me. I can't thank you enough, for now, I, too, am a woman of God.

Mom, I am so grateful that we are both still on this earth, and I have a chance to say, THANK YOU, for all of the life lessons you have instilled in me, Ronnie and Denise. You have always said that being a mother was your greatest joy, and you've done an excellent job of rearing us. I could not have asked for a better mother and friend. May God continue to bless and keep you.

Mom, I love you with all of my heart!

Danita

Danita Carter is a Chicago native and the alter-ego of Velvet and Sasha James. She also writes edgy novels for young adults. In addition to writing, Danita designs fine jewelry, and has enjoyed a successful career on Wall Street with several top financial institutions.

My Mother's Daughter
Valerie Wilson Wesley

Mommy. How long has it been since I've written that word? You've been dead for twenty-six years, and it's rare for me to say it. Most women my age call their mothers "Mom" and that was what I called you in my twenties, too embarrassed to say a name that made me feel like a little girl. An awkward "Mother" took the place of "Mom" in my thirties, although it never felt quite right with its air of haughtiness and distance, but it was perfect for a thirty-year-old determined to draw a line between herself and the woman who raised her.

Yet it was "Mommy" at forty when I sat on the edge of your bed listening to my sister read *The Mists of Avalon* as you fought the cancer that devoured you. Just saying Mommy—with all its dependence, vulnerability, unconditional love—reminded me then, and now, of who you were and will always be in my child-woman mind: maker of lemon frosting and afghans, fixer of feelings and broken toys, giver of dreams and pearl earrings. Mommy, despite all my running away, never left me.

Those months before your death were filled with turmoil—a marriage that was on the rocks, a writing career that was going nowhere—but the time I spent with you was filled with peace and joy though shadowed with dread. I had time to tell you how much I loved you, mumbled awkwardly as I lay beside you, unsure if you were awake and heard me, until you'd nod and say in your soft, husky voice that never crept beyond a whisper that you had. I know, you'd say, again and again. The sweet hoarseness of your voice floats back to me for an instant when I remember those moments, as does the quick, shy critical way you had of glancing at me, as if mystified by who I was.

I was a difficult child, challenging teenager and an aspiring writer, and writers, even developing ones, are notoriously hard to understand. I routinely challenged every bit of advice you offered, no matter how trivial, and you always seemed puzzled by my obstinacy. I suspected you would have preferred a different daughter, one who was more polite, ladylike, less opinionated, and that you hoped I'd become a teacher, lawyer, accountant—a sensible woman who made sensible decisions. One who could make a good living for herself, never be dependent on anybody else. For better or worse, a writer was what I became. I didn't realize how proud you were of me until after your death when I found the scrapbook you'd kept of my articles, each one cut and pasted on a page in the neat, methodical way you had of doing things.

You always kept your feelings tucked inside, close to your heart. Only a quick blink or subtle nod would let someone know what you were feeling. You were never completely comfortable with hugs—nobody in your family was. There was always a slight stiffening of your body when someone pulled you close, but the feelings were there—in your eyes and in that shy, self-conscious smile, as if you were afraid to show how deeply you loved. Your reticence could have come from the death of your sister, your beloved playmate, when you were a girl. Her death at twelve may have darkened your memory of childhood and made you fearful of loving too hard, holding too tightly. It was only with your grandchildren were you finally able to throw caution to the wind and embrace, hug, kiss with utter abandon. I understand now how fear of losing can make one wary of loving.

The older I get the more I grow into you. I look up sometimes and there you are—your eyes, my eyes, your smile, the one I never thought was mine, looks back at me from the bathroom mirror. Your touch is in the comfort foods I cook—potato salad, macaroni and cheese, pound cake; your deft hand controls mine. Your merriment comes out when I play with my grandson. Your funny expressions, rhymes, silly games, the rolling of eyes and giggle of voice. I adore him in the same inexpressibly deep way you loved my daughters. Your advice and mother wit are in my observations and spice up the dialogue of the characters in my stories.

A couple of years ago, I saw a picture taken at a New Year's Eve party and was struck by how much I looked like you. It was *your* slight smile that gazed back at me. Wow! I look like my mother, I said to my husband in amazement. You always have, he said.

It wasn't always so.

I was my father's daughter. I idolized him, and made no secret of it. I was like him in so many ways, same coloring, sense of humor, love of books, jazz, classical music. He loved to write and play the piano as much as I did. I was his favorite child and knew it, which was a heady, burdensome thing for a child to know. And you seemed willing to hand me over. You're just like your father, you'd murmur; a statement I'd heard from so many others it seemed indisputable. It's good luck to look like your father, people would tell me; the days of the patriarchy hadn't yet begun to fade so looking like your mother was never mentioned at all. You stayed in the shadows, letting your husband—my father—be the important one. He cooked the gourmet meals, told the amusing stories, threw the fancy parties. You lingered in the background, a slight, controlled smile on your lips.

Now in my sixties and after forty years of marriage, I realize what that did to you…and to me. The older I get, the more I understand the toll it must have taken. My father was not only a charming man but one of these guys impossible to rein in. He'd walk into a room and take it over; his laughter and high spirits ringing from every corner. He was irresistible to women; he knew it, and so did you. And like many successful men in his generation (in all generations), he was known and prone to stray, a poorly kept secret from both you and his daughters. He's been dead ten years, but I'm still saddened when I remember the small insults you put up with. How dependent you always seemed; how you valued his opinions above your own; how you allowed him to ridicule your family.

I can never judge you, him or your marriage, yet the more burnished your image becomes, the more tarnished his does. I understand now that if your pride rather than your practicality had ruled the day, you would have been faced with raising two daughters alone on a secretary's meager salary. And single motherhood was far less acceptable in the fifties and sixties than it is today.

You also understood your husband. He was a black man raised by a divorced mother living in a racist, segregated America where the stench of racism dogged every step he took, belittled his every word. Yet he managed to survive and be successful. He protected and provided for his family and made sure we thrived and wanted for nothing. He was a good man who gave us a good life. I will always love and admire him for that. And he adored you. I remember the expensive jewelry and clothes he bought for you on every occasion. Looking back though, I wonder if the gifts he chose were things he would have bought for himself if he'd been a woman— if he assumed his taste was yours. I wonder if he ever knew who *you* were.

I take pride now in your accomplishments which you never talked about. You was always so smart, even as a kid, my beloved uncle told me when you died. He spoke for you because you were never one to boast; you kept your successes to yourself, as well.

You never told me you were the only member of your family of twelve to go to college or how you dropped out to make money to send home. I knew how proud you were of being a secretary at a university, but never knew that you had accumulated fourteen months of sick time by the time you retired. You were a stickler for professionalism, I could see that. I remember teasing you about your "work voice" when I'd call you, and how you used to say, "I am the voice of the college—the only person some of them talk to." You were proud to be that.

After you died, I learned you had finished college in your spare time, making up for those years you'd lost, and that you were on the Board of Directors of one of the town's banks and for years had been an officer on the union board. I wish you'd told me that when you were alive so I could have celebrated you the way you deserved. Although you professed contentment with being "just a housewife, just a secretary," your true vocation was raising two daughters and urging them to go further than you did, to reach for that sun Zora Neale Hurston's people told her to aim for.

In two years, I'll be the same age you were when you died. I often think about your last days and about the grace with which you lived them. I remember the depth of love in your eyes when you said good-bye to me that morning and how you must have known you were dying even though I didn't. I was headed home that day, only to be called back as I walked into my house. I remember your last hours in the hospital, and how no one wanted to leave your side. Yours was a room packed full of family members who didn't want to let you go.

But we did and you were gone, and I was left only with myself. Thank you, Mommy, for the gift of your life…for the gift of mine.
Valerie

Valerie Wilson Wesley also writes under the name of Savana Welles. She was the recipient of the 2000 Award for Excellence in Adult Fiction from the Black Caucus of the American Library Association (BCALA). She is a graduate of Howard University and holds master's degrees from the Bank Street College of Education and the Columbia Graduate School of Journalism. She is married to noted screenwriter and playwright Richard Wesley and has two adult daughters.

My First Heroine
Tananarive Due

For the Due family—my mother, father and sisters, Johnita and Lydia—the year 2009 began with an epic high: the inauguration of President Barack Obama, the nation's first black president. My sisters and I had all flown in to my mother's hometown of Quincy, Florida, to watch the election results in November, and I still remember the stunning moment when the words *President-elect Barack Obama* appeared beneath his photo on the TV screen. My mother jumped and danced.

My sister Johnita and I joined my parents in Washington, D.C. on Inauguration Day, a family trip like no other. The bitter cold kept us indoors at the Newseum to watch it unfold on TV, but when we went to the rooftop, my mother was almost as excited to see her alma mater Florida A&M Marching 100 band stream below us on the street as she had been to see the new president's motorcade.

While she was a student at FAMU in 1960, my mother spent forty-nine days in jail for sitting in at a Woolworth lunch counter in Tallahassee, Florida, part of the nation's first Jail-In. She wore dark glasses her entire adult life after a police officer threw a teargas canister into her face during a peaceful protest march. She was arrested a dozen times for her civil rights work as far north as New York and as far south as Miami. She played trumpet as a music major before civil rights changed her life, though women weren't allowed in the Marching 100 when she was in school. Still, the schoolgirl was alive on her face as the band's dancing formation marched by.

My mother was the first heroine of my life. We grew up understanding that she and my father, civil rights attorney John Due, literally helped change the world. I co-authored a book with her, *Freedom in the Family: A Mother-Daughter Memoir of the Fight for Civil Rights.* She was my toughest taskmaster, hard to please, but she was my friend, my mirror, my role-model looming high above me, my impossible standard.

By the summer of 2009, my mother was suffering from such severe back pain that she spent much of her time in bed. In the fall, after a series of tests, she learned that she had Stage Four thyroid cancer that had spread to her spine. She spent months in the hospital and rehabilitation facilities.

She rallied by Mother's Day 2010 and had another year of a "normal" life, able to drive, travel and speak—she and my father even bought a house in Atlanta, closer to my sister. But she suffered a severe decline by the following Mother's Day, after an undiagnosed brain tumor was finally discovered, and suffered severe delusions and confusion that we had not expected to be a part of her illness.

As a family, we went to battle. We tried experts, treatments, prayers. But my father, sisters and I surrounded her at her bedside on the morning of February 7, 2012, singing freedom songs while we watched her take her last breath.

Her journey from strength to helplessness was so sudden that we had spent much of our energy working toward restoration rather than accepting that she would leave us. I remember hours at her bedside feeling like I was in a daze, not knowing what to say to her, wondering what she could understand. During that time, I often retreated to the game Angry Birds on my iPhone, trying to drive away the reality of how quickly our family had been turned upside down.

This is my letter to my mother.

Dear Mom:

I wonder what you would have thought of me then, if you'd come knocking on my dormitory door and convinced me to come to a civil rights meeting. I probably would have gone to the meeting, although, admittedly, I probably also would have missed a few. I probably would have been more afraid than you were. Maybe I would have lost my nerve when I saw the police lines waiting. Would the look of defiance like the one you wore on your face during your months of dying have given me the strength to keep marching?

Did you understand why it was so hard for me to find you where you had gone? Why I sometimes had so little to say? Did the game I played on my phone annoy you?

I know we were truly together at times—like the time you snapped from a stupor and sang freedom songs with Dad and me as if your life depended on it, as if the very sound of the music was your only window back to the world you had known. And you told me I had a sweet voice. And then there was the time I told you I would be teaching at Spelman College, and it was the last instant I knew you were proud of me.

Your anger frightened me. Your anger always had frightened me. I never met you before the teargas and jail cells, but I know your anger was never far from you by the time we were a family. Your anger, like your dark glasses, was one of your scars.

"Mom," I said at your bedside one day, "do you know my name?"

"Tananarive Priscilla Asshole Due," you said. I can laugh only now. (Was it you, or was it your anger?)

"I used to be quite fond of you," you'd said another time from your bed, staring earnestly into my eyes, "but something has changed."

Like author Octavia E. Butler tried to teach us, "The only lasting Truth is change."

Your dying was a wall between us I never felt that I learned how to climb.

But our only lasting truth is that you loved your children fiercely, and we worshipped you. You taught us our history so we would know who we were and from whence we had come. You taught us to care about the plight of others. You taught us the importance of honesty and courage. You taught me to be a storyteller.

And as you always said, we were so used to seeing you as strong that we often could not recognize when you needed help. And sometimes you had trouble asking for it.

And in the end, you called my sister "Mommy." You needed us to hold your hand and mother you and cover you with the lilac blanket with pink flowers we brought you.

And we had to learn to let go of the names, the words, the titles, the memories, the expectations, the worries, and simply Be.

We had to let go.

Tananarive Due is the Cosby Chair in the Humanities at Spelman College in Atlanta, Georgia. The author and screenwriter has written a dozen novels and a civil rights memoir and has won an American Book Award and NAACP Image Award. She is married to author Steven Barnes and is raising a son, Jason.

Couldn't Have Asked for More
Zane

Dear Lib,

I am not going to say "Dear Mom" because I have never called you that. I fell into the mix with my three older siblings who always called you by your nickname, Lib, short for Elizabeth, from day one. So no need to change for this book. The fact that you did that showed that you and our father planned to have a closeness to us that was slightly different than normal. The two of you gave all four of us an outstanding, educational, and enlightening childhood.

From my earliest memories, age three, all I can recall is strength, determination, respect, and compassion that you have had for everyone under the sun. No one was going to feel left out on your watch, from the numerous coworkers that you hosted birthday, retirement, and baby shower events for to the students and dozens of "adopted" nieces and nephews that you placed upon your heart. Many of them had no one else to celebrate their milestones in life. You recognized that and sacrificed your time, money, and effort to make them feel good about themselves.

I called them "events" instead of "parties" because that is exactly what they were, and will continue to be since you are still hosting them on the regular. From the elaborate decorations, venues, and planned-out programs that always include an acrostic or poem written by you in their honor, you are truly an entertainer. That is where I get it from and it has been a pleasure to pick up the torch. Everyone often asks me how I can cook enough food for fifty to a hundred people with seamless effort. It is because I watched you do it for so long. Now that you are older, you plan the events and I execute them. We make an amazing team.

I often say that I do not have any negative memories of my parents and that is true. I have never seen you and my father argue, yell, or even talk down about one another. Surely, there have been trying moments, but you both somehow managed to mask them or protect us from it. I am eternally grateful for being provided such a stable environment in my youth. Many of my friends were not as blessed and grew up in complete dysfunction. Most of them came to you to talk about their issues; they did not feel comfortable discussing it with their own mothers for fear of being misjudged, ridiculed, punished, or ignored altogether.

You are a magnificent woman and I could not have spoken a greater mother into existence. No matter how many times I changed my mind about what I wanted to do in my youth, i.e., soccer, ballet, dance, tap, guitar, clarinet, drums, art, etc., you were always open to letting me try it. I did not stick with most of them, but I enjoyed them all immensely. Having the freedom to express myself creatively, no matter what, where or when, is the main reason why I am who I am today.

I was mad when you made me take speed reading in third grade, but when I started reading a book daily in sixth grade, I was delighted that I could abandon reality and get lost in the minds of fiction writers. I was mad when you told me that I could not go to high school in a crime-infested neighborhood and was shipped off to an elite high school in Atlanta the day before school started. Again, it was a blessing. Everything you ever did for me was a blessing. And in return, I have a much greater understanding of how to raise children myself. While I allow my children to express themselves as well, I also recognize when it is time to give a final answer and stick to it.

On a daily basis I receive dozens of emails from females who were raised in chaos, pain, confusion, and violence. You never laid a finger on me and I appreciate that. So many believe that children have to receive "whoopings" and be beaten into submission in order to become responsible adults. My siblings and I are all clear-cut examples that that is not true. In return, I have never hit my children either, and they are the most loving, brilliant human beings that I have never known.

Even though you are my mother, I have always regarded you as my closest and dearest friend. There has never been anything that I had to feel uncomfortable discussing with you, even if it did not paint me in the most positive of lights. I have made a ton of mistakes, bad choices, and have shared the ultimate tragedy with you since we both lost children that we loved dearly. Being able to express my pain to you during the time of the loss of my first daughter, and having you be able to relate to it, was a godsend. I watched you endure the death of my brother and you were hurt, but you made sure that you were strong for your living children. I had to follow that same example when it seemed so much easier to give up.

I would be remiss not to thank you for my faith and spirituality. Without it, I would have given up a long time ago instead of real-izing that it is better to let go and let God. Sure, we all have to be proactive in life, but there is a time when we must understand that only God can step in and make the necessary change. You and my father made sure that, as a child, I was exposed to all different types of people, cultures, and religions. It was hard to understand why back then but I know why now. You did that so that we would be able to embrace the differences in people instead of fearing them. So that we would not fall into the ugly, generational curse of judging people solely on the color of their skin, their background, or their beliefs. You taught us to respect the opinions of others and not take it personally. That everyone is simply a culmination of all that they have been taught, experienced, and observed.

Back when I was in college, you gave me a book that solidified a lot of things for me. I do not recall the name but I remember all of the content. It was about how women allow drama to dictate their lives, to stifle their growth, and block their blessings. It was a true eye-opener. The takeaway from it was that drama is a dream killer. So many women believe that relationships are not normal or healthy if they are not plagued with arguments, hesitation, and insecurity. Unfortunately, many grow up watching their mothers be hurt by man after man until they equate physical, emotional, and economic abuse with love. They believe that they can never do better; that they can never live the fairytale.

On the flip side, I have always believed in fairytales. I still do to this very day. I realize that it is not about continuously searching for men who serve as additional examples of what a good man should not be, but only entertaining men who can be "the example" of what a good man should be. In return, I am instilling those same beliefs in my own daughter, your namesake. Thank God that you made me realize my worth at an early age so that I could turn around and make sure that she realized hers. You always made me feel like I was special, like I was different, and that I deserved the world laid at my feet. That is why, to this day, I call my own daughter Princess and tell her how beautiful she is so that she will never rely solely on a man to validate that for her. She understands that men will always be readily available once she gets her life in order and that already being established makes embarking on a toxin-free relationship even better.

I have watched you be treated like a queen my entire life and now my kids call me "Queen Diva Mother." My father has cherished you for sixty years; most women will never be able to say that. I want to thank you for being the pillar of strength, grace, and humanity in my life. If I had been born to someone else, my heart might not be in the same place. Day in and day out, I witness women attack each other verbally, trying to uplift themselves by demeaning someone else. That never occurred in our house or even in our presence. You and your friends were like bona fide sisters and it showed in every cookout, gathering, or celebration that all of the families engaged in together.

I must thank you for being my biggest supporter and fan. To this day, I still give you the first copy of every book, hot off the presses. Without you helping me out with the kids, I would not be able to do half of the things that I do; not even a quarter. You have been my protector, my confidante, and my backbone in many things and I truly love and appreciate you. I cherish you more than any other.

There are really no words that can totally express how I feel about you. It would take a 120,000-word tome to even capture it all. So let me simply say this: Some people never get to meet their heroes. Mine gave birth to me.

Love,
Zane

Zane is the New York Times bestselling author of dozens of titles. She is the publisher of Strebor Books, an imprint of Atria/Simon & Schuster. She is the creator, executive producer and scriptwriter of Cinemax's Zane's The Jump Off *and* Zane's Sex Chronicles. *She lives in the Washington, D.C. area.*

A Golden Heart
Charmaine R. Parker

When I look at vintage photos of my mother, they depict a charming young woman, well-groomed with thick, gorgeous hair—a future schoolteacher in the South. As a child visiting my maternal grandparents and relatives in North Carolina, I savored the open spaces and laid-back lifestyle. I experienced ongoing hospitality and warmth in contrast to the fast-paced environment of Washington, D.C. where I was raised.

Despite the sometimes cold nature of the city, our home was full of love. My parents, both educators, stressed the importance of education and travel. Our basement was a library with a massive book collection. It was there where I gained my love for literature, whether it was from the mysteries I'd received from children's book clubs or the urban novels I later discovered as a teen in my dad's personal collection. I am grateful that reading and writing were viewed as a way of life.

My mother, who calls herself "Poetess," and my father, a scholar and prolific author, both influenced me as a writer. I started crafting poetry, skits and short stories, in elementary school. Later, I would have a lifelong career with words. My first job was as a proofreader. After graduate school, I entered the world of journalism as a reporter and editor. This would lead to roles as publishing director and novelist.

I always wondered how my mother could teach a classroom of elementary children and then return home to four of her own.

She always managed to hold down the fort, even when my dad traveled throughout the country and the world. Traveling was a major part of my upbringing and looking back, I realize even more now that I was truly blessed with the opportunity. Whether it was overlooking the Grand Canyon, Niagara Falls or the San Francisco Bay, I saw few children who looked like me. All of the educational places we explored offered me a well-rounded perspective with a wide outlook on life. It shaped me as a child and as an adult. In turn, when I became a mother, I emulated what my parents had taught and ensured my daughter would see the world.

Growing up in D.C., once nicknamed "Chocolate City," I appreciated the experiences a cosmopolitan lifestyle offered. You could easily become engrossed in the party scene as a teen and young adult. There was so much happening and places to go that were attractive. My mother once said and I often quote: "You need to do something cultural for a change." Those words stuck and I've lived my life with them in mind. Travel and culture are a priority.

My mother has a huge heart and an uplifting personality. Her kindness is praised as she lives by the word "giving." And she gives freely, openly and genuinely with love. If someone is ill, she takes time to send a card. If someone requests one of her mouth-watering apple or peach cobblers, she blends the ingredients and rolls out the dough with care. If someone needs words of encouragement, she finds a book or writes her own inspirational message. If there is a special event, she uses her creativity and makes a gift or writes an acrostic, poem or song.

Recently, we were talking and ironically, it was about the nature of giving and how some may never offer invitations. She shared that her mother always said, "Don't be on the receiving end." The statement clicked, how true. Then she added, "That was her motto."

It was the first time I'd heard the expression from the one-time cookout guru who was always entertaining. If it wasn't in our back-yard or at home, it was at the park. She, too, has lived her life through her mother's words.

My mother has lived eighty-six years as a blessed and healthy person. Medical professionals are amazed that she doesn't own prescriptions. The Lord is her medicine. It's fascinating how she manages to maintain the calendar of a thirty-year-old. It constantly is overflowing with events, meetings, luncheons and programs. She strives to attend as many sorority, alumni, history and women's group meetings as possible. Her energy transcends her age and she has more than enough to spread. I often jokingly say that her sched-ule is fuller than my own—and that's busy. When she's not on the run, then she's occupied between crosswords and TV game shows.

Through her strength and caring attitude, she is often treated as the matriarch of our extended family. Her only sister, my ninety-five-year-old Aunt Rose, is her twin in spirit and love. The duo fearlessly assists family members and friends and supports their communities. Surely, this is a trickle-down effect as my dear grand-mother, who lived to be in her nineties, was also a matriarch. The three of them exemplify a team of traditional giving and thought-fulness.

If it hadn't been for my mother teasing her nephew about him staying in L.A. and not returning to the East Coast, I doubt I ever would have stayed. Once she proposed the notion, I seriously gave it some thought myself. Why was I going back home? I couldn't come up with a viable reason, other than missing my family and friends. So I made a life-changing decision and let the family make the cross-country trip without me while I settled on the West Coast. I didn't hop in the car that day and those four years were crucial in my coming of age as an adult. Her words sparked a spontaneous decision that would positively affect my life.

My Dearest "Lib,"

From day one, we've always addressed you as "Lib," short for Elizabeth. We never called you "Mom," "Mommy" or "Mother." It may be unusual, but it never meant that you did not reflect the full essence of motherhood.

It is a pleasure to write to you to tell you how much I love you. Your compassion is forever appreciated. Your support is endless.

I thank you for showing me the way: how to be strong, confident and live my life to the fullest. By your example, I strive to lead my daughter in a positive light.

You are a treasured mother, wife, grandmother, aunt, godmother, cousin, mother-in-law, friend, confidante, soror, and the list goes on.

Your creativity is exuded when you recite an original rap at family reunions or create an artistic collage as a birthday gift. Your cooking skills are displayed when you whip up a delicious, home-cooked meal—you were able to do at age twelve—or prepare cobblers that folks declare are the best they've ever tasted. Your dedication is shown when you give back to the community as a volunteer tutor of schoolchildren or when you bring the family together for special occasions, especially birthdays. Your kindness is depicted when you make an extra effort to offer words of wisdom or place a friendly call to brighten someone's day. Your humorous nature is witnessed when you are the first to the dance floor at a wedding reception or when you tease in an attempt to play relationship matchmaker.

Behind your sweet nature, you also know how to state what you have to say, be upfront when necessary and keep it moving—with grace. It is an admirable quality.

I appreciate you raising us to be real. Although you were a minister's wife and we were preacher's children (or PK's, preacher's kids), your view of the world was not stifling. Perhaps you always managed to stay in tune with change and trends through your teaching career, being in touch with the youth over the thirty-plus years in the classroom. You and Dad kept up with the times and accepted transition.

Reflecting on my life, you insisted I take typing class during night school (I can't thank you enough as every job I've ever had required typing skills.) You ensured you enrolled me in tap, ballet, piano and sewing lessons. At the same time, you were aware that in addition to the cultural skills, social life was important. My closest friends and I will forever remember and be grateful for all the R&B concert tickets you provided us. They were a joy for teenage girls who lost their voices as screaming fans.

Thank you for shaping me into the person I am and for being a wonderful role model, not only for me but for your granddaughter. Thank you for always having a listening ear. You are truly a pillar of strength.

I only hope that this apple hasn't fallen far from the tree.

I *L-O-V-E* you.

Charmaine

Charmaine R. Parker is the author of The Trophy Wives *and* The Next Phase of Life. *She started writing fiction and poetry during early childhood. She has a bachelor's degree in fine arts from Howard University and a master's degree in print journalism from the University of Southern California. Born in North Carolina, she was raised in Washington, D.C. Currently a Maryland resident, she is married and has one daughter. Visit the author on Facebook / Charmaine Roberts Parker and Twitter @Charmainebooks.*

Beyond the Corner of My Eye
Nina Foxx

I only have very hazy memories of my mother. I remember her sweeping the floor with a yellow broom. I remember the hem of her dress. I remember her asking me what I wanted to be when I grew up.

"A psychologist," I replied. I was less than seven when I said that. She didn't live to my eighth birthday.

I remember her fighting with my father for whatever reason, then storming out of the house. She would always take me with her, but she would leave my younger brother. She'd tell my father that he could have the boy, and the two of us would go, in her Corvette, I think it was yellow, and drive. We wouldn't go far. Each time, we ended up at Baisley Park in Jamaica, Queens. We'd sit there until a cop told us to leave; sometimes it was getting dark, and then we'd go home again. I know now from family stories that she knew she was dying long before I was even cognizant of myself, and she was angry about it.

Other memories of her include her and me in the neighborhood bar in the morning and her hanging on a fence, drunk, by the back of her shirt with me standing by her side, waiting with her while one of her drinking buddies went to get my father. My mother tried to drown the pain of her impending death. I don't think it worked.

Until I started to ask people to write the letters in this book, I never gave much thought to what I would say to my own mother

had I the chance. I thought I had no feelings toward her whatso-
ever; as far as I could recall, it had really only ever been my father
and my brother and me, living in the shadow of my father's memory
of her. I thought I had nothing to say. I realize now that the words
were just not ready to come.

Mommy,

I still think of you as my Mommy, as a small child would. You
are frozen in my head that way, your hair flopping down in my
face when you woke me, your smell, the way you called me when
you came in from the night shift at the hospital and woke me in
the morning. Just shadows are all that remain of the short time
we had together. I know of you through the people who knew you
better than me; your brothers, Grandma, even Daddy's other
daughters seem to have had more of you than I did. I know of you
through the things in that they say remind me of you.

People loved you. And from that, I know that you would have
loved me. You tried to take care of me in your absence. That woman
you chose to be our babysitter (they didn't call them nannies then)
while you were sick? She took care of us until I was fifteen years
old. It was not an ideal situation, by any means, but now I can
honestly say that I had a British nanny until I was fifteen. It sounds
more glamorous than it was.

There are so many times when I was sure you were watching. I
spent years looking for glimpses of your spirit from the corner of
my eye. Grandma told me that sometimes, when the veil was thin,
you could see people who had crossed to the other side, and children
she said were especially good at this. Every time the sitter was
mean to me or to my brother, I looked for you, sure that you were
watching over us. I checked behind me for many years, and some-

times I still do. I know that you didn't want to leave me. As a mother, I know that no mother wants to leave her young children. The veil is always thin for me, and to this day, I can sometimes feel you watching me.

Mommy, Brian got us out of there, not me. I failed there. I was supposed to be the big sister, the protector, but instead, I somehow had incredible patience. I was just the one who waited for things to pass. I was too scared about doing the right thing, so I did nothing. He was the one that blew up and acted crazy and then the woman didn't want to take care of us anymore. That was fitting. You see, I think the sitter sensed his impatience. Over the years, he was the one that was on the receiving end of much of her callousness, not me. My patience saved me from that. She knew that any coldness or meanness would be lost on me; losing my mother left me with a very thick skin and a very long fuse.

I did learn some things from her though. I learned that I hate plastic on furniture. The way my thighs would stick to it when I tried to get up made my skin crawl. I took from her a love of Cream of Wheat in the morning with one slice of toast, and a need for a daily cup of English-style tea. She believed that idle hands do the devil's work, so I learned to knit (I can knit just about anything and make it look like it came from a store) and my brother—he resisted learning anything from her at all.

Us leaving there was for the better. The whole thing caused a huge family fight. I really only found this out after the fact, when I wrote a book about it and let people in the family read it. It was actually a relief to find out how they felt. I felt more loved afterward, to know that this choice you and Daddy made wasn't a popular one. After he died, my sister told me that he really thought he was doing the right thing. By having her take care of us in his absence, he felt he was raising his children himself, even though his absences grew longer and longer. At least we were close, not across town or across the country with Grandma. And the two of us, my brother and me, were together.

It was very painful to write that book and it took me years. I cried sometimes when I was writing the chapters, blending my six-year-old memories with that of other people in the family so that I could tell the fullest story possible. I bled on the page over at least nine years, but when I was done, things were better. It was if writing it all down somehow left me less empty.

For a long time after you died, Daddy didn't do well. Things were a mess. He worked all the time (as he probably had to do), and it was years before he cleaned your stuff out of the closets. You were everywhere. It was like he was frozen for a bit. We all were. And although he started to date, he didn't really attach to anyone in any meaningful way until years later. And that was interesting. She looked like you. Funny thing is, she knew it, too. I called her on it and she admitted it. She was the type of woman that was grateful to live in another woman's shadow. Today, twenty years after Daddy's death, we don't speak. We shunned her like she was an Amish outcast.

By the time she came along, I was just about grown. She moved in and tried to take over the best she could. She was chosen; that was her right. I didn't really live with her for any long period of time, but she showed me that as a woman, you have to stand up for what you want.

We kept going to see your mother in Alabama every summer until she died. Daddy would ship us out right after school got out. Those summers were free and normal and good. It was there that I learned how much like you I am. Apparently you had a mind of your own and did whatever you wanted to do. I think you gave that to me. Thank you. I certainly am adventurous. Your death taught me that you only live once so I might as well enjoy it, and when I visited Grandma in Bessemer, I did.

Just so you know, I think growing up without you made me a better mother. After my first child was born, I realized that it was important for her to know that she would be okay without me if it ever came to that. As a result I made her go to camp, even though I cried leaving her and kept calling the counselors to check in on her. I gave her many situations where she had to be independent as I was forced to be. She's adventurous now, too, and quite independent. You would enjoy both of the girls. They are both like me in different ways. The older one is very strong and thoughtful. She has far more will to say no and stand her ground than I did when I was her age. I think she is like I am now. The younger one is willful and determined, and although I'm sure that will give me hell when she is in her teen years, I'm positive it will serve her well as an adult. I tell them both my few stories of you often so that they will know you in their hearts.

Through the years, there were many times when people gave me the pity eyes or said things like "how would she know how to do that? She doesn't have a mother." I went from angry to just ignoring then. After a while, I realized I should have been the one saying to them, how would you know how I am or will be? You have never been in my situation. Be assured though, you left me in a strong village. The women in my life guided me expertly.

I got so many good things from your mother. Although we were far away, we were close. Before email and long distance telephone, I wrote old-fashioned letters to her often.

Various girlfriends of Daddy's left me with different things. There were, or course, those who were nice and those who were nice only because they thought it would make their trip to the altar easier. I could always spot them. There was only one really (and not the one he attached to) who impacted my life.

She went to Concord Baptist Church, where Daddy's family went when he was younger. I'm not sure if that is how they met, though. They eventually went their separate ways, but I liked her and followed her life until she died. She taught me that if I act like I belong, no one will ever question me, and for the most part, she was right. Unfortunately, I think she was the jealous type, so eventually, that relationship petered out.

Mommy, I think you would be happy to know that most of my "mother" gifts came from a place much closer to home. When I was a kid and needed to be rescued from the sitter so I could just play outside like other kids, it was Lynda, Daddy's daughter, who rescued me. We would go and spend the weekend with her and her husband. Brian and I were her children before she had any. She scooped me up, embraced me and mothered me in the most sisterly way she could. She was there when I needed advice, giving it even when I didn't want it. When I got married, she was there for me. When I had kids, she was there for me. She dried my tears and held my hand.

When I wanted to quit graduate school before it had even started, she helped me pack my things to trek back across the country while reminding me that I would be okay since Walmart was hiring. I'm sure Walmart is a fine place to work, but it would have been a far cry from the psychologist that little-girl me had told you I wanted to be. Because of her, I did what I had to do every day, wearing a dead man's coat that I bought from a secondhand store in Chelsea. She is the reason I steeled myself when a racist professor made me travel over an hour with no money to make copies for him. She held my hand when I cried about that professor antagonizing me by asking if I was sure my single father was "a black" since it was "so unusual" for him to have had the ability to raise us alone.

She's my friend, and I believe we will be friends forever. She and Robert went from being my sister and her husband to my other-mother and my other-dad. No one can ever replace you, but she has come damned close to filling the hole that was left when you died, reminding me every step that you are with me, somewhere just beyond the corner of my eye.

Nina

Nina Foxx is an award-winning filmmaker, playwright and novelist. She writes as both Nina Foxx and Cynnamon Foster and has authored eight novels, contributed to several anthologies and co-authored a text on writing. Nina and her younger brother were raised by a single father in New York City.